Representing Employees of Intergovernmental Organizations and Their Spouses in Divorce

LESLIE MILLER AND JESSICA MARKHAM

AMERICAN BAR ASSOCIATION
Family Law Section

Cover design by Sara Wadford/ABA Design

Printed in the United States of America.

29 28 27 26 25 5 4 3 2 1

ISBN 978-1-63905-669-9

Contents

Acknowledgments

Leslie Miller: Jessica Markham came up with the idea for this book, and in a brilliant move of delegation convinced me to take the lead on the first draft. Her reviews, edits, and reorganization of this book throughout the process have been instrumental to describing these complex plans and benefits as simply as possible. As a mentor over these 13 years, she has taught me how to write better, explain simpler, and question more, all skills without which this book would not have been completed (and all of which are consistently being worked on). Jillian Morris pushing me to believe in myself (and set and meet deadlines) gave me the necessary motivation to get this across the finish line. But most of all, I want to acknowledge my husband Anthony, for consistently believing that I could learn these plans, figure out a way to explain them, and make them more easily understandable to those who need the information. His support over the months of research, writing, and frustration got me through any moments of doubting whether this book would ever get done.

Jessica Markham: First and foremost, I want to thank my co-author, Leslie, for doing way more than her fair share on this book. Also, for mostly always saying yes to my ideas and doing a super hard thing, which was stay awake while writing this book. I also want to thank her in advance for answering any and all questions about this book. Second, I want to note that in my first book I thanked a lot of people, but I missed one big one. So, to quote Snoop Dogg, I now say: "I want to thank me for believing in me, I want to thank me for doing all this hard work. I wanna thank me for having no days off. I wanna thank me for never quitting. I wanna thank me for always being a giver and trying to give more than I receive. I wanna thank me for trying to do more right than wrong. I wanna thank me for being me at all times, [Jessica Markham], you a bad m*********er."

Acknowledgments

About the Authors

Leslie Miller focuses her practice in the areas of complex retirement divisions and the preparation of qualified domestic relations orders. She is frequently retained by attorneys in the DC Metro area and beyond to assist in their complex retirement matters as co-counsel or expert witness. She is licensed to practice law in Maryland, Washington, D.C., and Virginia. Ms. Miller received her JD from the University of Baltimore, School of Law. While at the University of Baltimore, Ms. Miller served as a staff editor and then as the manuscript editor for Law Forum. Ms. Miller has received numerous honors, including having been selected for inclusion as a "Rising Star" by *Maryland SuperLawyers Magazine* and *DC SuperLawyers Magazine*. Ms. Miller is active in various local bar associations, including the Women's Bar Association of Maryland, Frederick & Montgomery Counties, the District of Columbia Bar, and the Maryland State Bar Association, holding various leadership positions. She was selected as a Fellow of the "Bar Leaders" of the Montgomery County Bar Foundation and a Fellow of the Maryland State Bar Foundation. Ms. Miller regularly presents continuing legal education and public and private courses to attorneys on the subject of retirement.

Jessica Markham is a family attorney in private practice based in Bethesda, Maryland, and Washington, D.C. Ms. Markham and the members of her firm, Markham Law Firm (www.markhamlegal.com) practice all aspects of family law. Ms. Markham has prepared hundreds of retirement court orders, and frequently consults on retirement issues. She has extensive trial experience but advocates settlement over the adversarial process of litigation and is also trained in collaborative law. Ms. Markham also has an active mediation practice, helping parties to resolve divorce-related disputes as a neutral, and is frequently appointed as a mediator by local courts.

Ms. Markham has been recognized by her peers for her work. She is a Fellow of the American Bar Foundation and the Maryland State Bar Foundation. Since 2018, Ms. Markham has been recognized by her peers for inclusion in "The Best Lawyers in America" in the field of family law for the Washington, D.C., area, and the firm was recognized as a Best Firm in 2019 and 2020. Ms. Markham was named a Top Divorce Lawyer (Divorce) by *Washingtonian Magazine* and Top Attorney by *Bethesda Magazine* (Family Law and ADR). Markham has also received numerous honors including the Martindale-Hubbell Peer Review Rating of AV Preeminent in the field of family law, and inclusion in Maryland SuperLawyers and Washington DC Super-Lawyers Magazines. Ms. Markham is the author of the American Bar Association book published March 2021, *Representing Federal Employees and Their Spouses in Divorce: A Practical Guide.*

Preface

This book provides guidance for the family law practitioner handling a case that involves a current or former employee of certain intergovernmental organizations. The information is critical to representing the interests of your client no matter what side you're on. By reading this book, you will know what important issues to look out for. This book will flag issues, give you information you need to handle the matter yourself, or allow you to know when to consult an expert. An attorney at any level of practice will find valuable information here that is of critical use in such cases. Each section starts with the basics and moves to the most detailed aspects, and highlights practice pointers you can flip to later as needed.

While it is impossible to touch on all relevant case law throughout the country that touches on these topics, we have included relevant citations and major case law for some jurisdictions. We have attempted to make this information accessible, and we have included various checklists, glossary terms, and definitions. This book will help you negotiate or try a case to reach the best possible outcome where these issues are at play.

Introduction

Defining Intergovernmental Organizations

The intergovernmental organizations discussed in this book are some of the international organizations impacting, creating, supporting, and enforcing international laws. These organizations are also sometimes referred to as world treaty organizations. A country's participation in any intergovernmental organization is voluntary and occasionally requires the approval of the existing members to join. Each has its own mission statement and goals of the issues it seeks to address.

The authority for the United States to join an intergovernmental organization lies in the Constitution. Pursuant to Article II, Section II, the president has "Power, by and with the Advice and Consent of the Senate, to make Treaties, provided two thirds of the Senators present concur[.]" The president or his representative may sign on to treaties first and then submit the treaty to the Senate for ratification. The president's signature on the treaty before being ratified by the Senate is an expression of willingness of the signing country to continue the treaty-making process and creates an obligation to refrain in good faith from taking any actions that would defeat the purpose of the treaty.[1] Once ratified, the country is making an intentional act to be bound by the treaty.[2]

This book covers the following organizations:

1. International Monetary Fund (IMF)
2. Inter-American Development Bank (IDB)
3. International Bank for Reconstruction and Development (World Bank)
4. United Nations (UN)

---

1. Vienna Convention on the Law of Treaties 1969, Articles 10 and 18.
2. *Id.* Article 2.

The following is a list of public international organizations of which the United States is a member by treaty or statute within the meaning of sections 316(b) or 319(b) of the International Organizations Immunities Act (described further in this Introduction under Privileges and Immunities):

African Development Bank (E.O. 12403, Feb. 8, 1983)

African Development Fund (E.O 11977, Mar. 14, 1977)

Asian Development Bank (E.O. 11334, Mar. 7, 1967)

Caribbean Organization (E.O. 10983, Dec. 30, 1961)

Criminal Police Organization (E.O. 12425, June 16, 1983)

Customs Cooperation Council (E.O. 11596, June 5, 1971)

European Space Research Organization (ESRO) (E.O. 11760, Jan. 17, 1974)

Food and Agriculture Organization, The (E.O. 9698, Feb 19, 1946)

Great Lakes Fishery Commission (E.O. 11059, Oct. 23, 1962)

Inter-American Defense Board (E.O. 10228, Mar. 26, 1951)

Inter-American Development Bank (E.O. 10873, Apr. 8, 1960)

Inter-American Institute for Cooperation on Agriculture (E.O. 9751, July 11, 1946)

Inter-American Statistical Institute (E.O. 9751, July 11, 1946)

Inter-American Tropical Tuna Commission (E.O. 11059, Oct. 23, 1962)

Intergovernmental Committee for European Migration (formerly the Provisional Intergovernmental Committee for the Movement of Migrants from Europe) (E.O. 10335, Mar. 28, 1952)

Intergovernmental Maritime Consultative Organization (E.O 10795, Dec. 13, 1958)

International Atomic Energy Agency (E.O. 10727, Aug. 31, 1957)

International Bank for Reconstruction and Development (E.O. 9751, July 11, 1946)

International Centre for Settlement of Investment Disputes (E.O. 11966, Jan. 19, 1977)

International Civil Aviation Organization (E.O. 9863, May 31, 1947)

International Coffee Organization (E.O. 11225, May 22, 1965)

International Cotton Advisory Committee (E.O. 9911, Dec. 19, 1947)

International Development Association (E.O. 11966, Jan. 19, 1977)

International Fertilizer Development Center (E.O. 11977, Mar. 14, 1977)

International Finance Corporation (E.O. 10680, Oct. 2, 1956)

International Food Policy Research Institute (E.O. 12359, Apr. 22, 1982)

International Hydrographic Bureau (E.O. 10769, May 29, 1958)

International Hydrographic Bureau (E.O. 10769, May 29, 1958)

International Institute for Cotton (E.O. 11283, May 27, 1966)

International Institute for Cotton (E.O. 11283, May 27, 1966)

International Joint Commission—United States and Canada (E.O. 9972, June 25, 1948

International Joint Commission—United States and Canada (E.O. 9972, June 25, 1948)

International Labor Organization, The (functions through staff known as The International Labor Office) (E.O. 9698, Feb. 19, 1946)

International Labor Organization, The (functions through staff known as The International Labor Office) (E.O. 9698, Feb. 19, 1946)

International Maritime Satellite Organization (E.O. 12238, Sept. 12, 1980)

International Monetary Fund (E.O. 9751, July 11, 1946)

International Pacific Halibut Commission (E.O. 11059, Oct. 23, 1962)

International Secretariat for Volunteer Service (E.O. 11363, July 20, 1967)

International Telecommunications Satellite Organization (INTELSAT) (E.O. 11718, May 14, 1973)

International Telecommunication Union (E.O. 9863, May 31, 1947)

International Wheat Advisory Committee (E.O. 9823, Jan. 24, 1947)

Multinational Force and Observers (E.O. 12359, Apr. 22, 1982)

Organization for European Economic Cooperation (E.O. 10133, June 27, 1950) (Now known as Organization for Economic Cooperation and Development; 28 FR 2959, Mar. 26, 1963)

Organization of African Unity (OAU) (E.O. 11767, Feb. 19, 1974)

Organization of American States (includes Pan American Union) (E.O. 10533, June 3, 1954)

Pan American Health Organization (includes Pan American Sanitary Bureau) (E.O. 10864, Feb. 18, 1960)

Preparatory Commission for the International Refugee Organization and its successor, the International Refugee Organization (E.O. 9887, Aug. 22, 1947)

Preparatory Commission of the International Atomic Energy Agency (E.O. 10727, Aug. 31, 1957)

South Pacific Commission (E.O. 10086, Nov. 25, 1949)

United International Bureau for the Protection of Intellectual Property (BIRPI) (E.O. 11484, Sept. 29, 1969)

United Nations, The (E.O. 9698, Feb. 19, 1946)

United Nations Educational, Scientific, and Cultural Organizations (E.O. 9863, May 31, 1947)

Universal Postal Union (E.O. 10727, Aug. 31, 1957)

World Health Organization (E.O. 10025, Dec. 30, 1948)

World Intellectual Property Organization (E.O. 11866, June 18, 1975)

World Meteorological Organization (E.O. 10676, Sept. 1, 1956)

What Are the Benefits That Are Divisible in Divorce?

The intergovernmental organizations discussed in this book have retirement benefits that can be divided upon the divorce of an employee/retiree and their (former) spouse. Some also have life insurance policies that can be assigned, or health insurance policies that can be continued for a period of time after the divorce. Others also provide additional benefits such as contribution toward education (including college) expenses for the parties' children and funds for the family to visit the family's home country during the employment period. Although such additional benefits may not be divisible by the court in the parties' divorce, they might be useful in negotiations and future financial planning for your client and their family.

History of Intergovernmental Organizations

The earliest intergovernmental organizations known in modern history were formed to regulate river navigation on the Rhine and Danube rivers in the 1800s.[3] Other organizations dealing with technology were formed later in the century with the boom of the industrial revolution.[4] In the 1890s, many organizations were formed to promote peace, including the Hague Conference of 1899 which adopted the Convention for the Pacific Settlement of International Disputes and the Hague Conference of 1907 which created the Permanent Court of Arbitration.[5] This movement led to the creation of the more than 300 intergovernmental organizations in existence today.[6]

---

3. The United Nations Office at Geneva, *Historical Background of the League of Nations*, https://www.ungeneva.org/en/about/league-of-nations/background#:~:text=Although%20the%20first%20international%20organizations,Measures%20(1875)%2C%20and%20the (last visited May 1, 2025). Referencing the Central Commission for the Navigation on the Rhine formed in 1815, and the Danube Commission formed in 1856.

4. *Id.*

5. *Id.*

6. Nat'l Geographic Soc'y, *International Organization*, https://education.nationalgeographic.org/resource/international-organization/ (last visited May 1, 2025).

The end of World War I brought about the creation of the League of Nations when the Treaty of Versailles came into force on January 10, 1920.[7] The United States refused to ratify the treaty and support for the League declined and the League was largely ineffective. With the onset of World War II, there was a need for an effective international organization to help resolve disputes on a large scale.[8]

In July 1944, delegates from 44 nations gathered in Bretton Woods, New Hampshire, to agree on post-war cooperation.[9] The result of the conference was the drafting of the governing documents for the International Monetary Fund and the International Bank for Reconstruction and Development.[10]

During the early 1940s, a series of charters, declarations, and conferences resulted in the 1944 San Francisco Conference and the drafting of the United Nations Charter.[11]

Similarly, the First Pan-American Conference occurred in 1890 and discussions for an inter-American system throughout Latin America began.[12] Finally, in 1959, the Organizations of American States drafted the Articles of Agreement to form the Inter-American Development Bank.[13]

---

7. The United Nations Office at Geneva, *supra* note 3.

8. U.S. Dep't of State, Office of the Historian, *League of Nations, 1920*, https://history.state.gov/milestones/1914-1920/league#:~:text=The%20League%20of%20Nations%20was,forum%20for%20resolving%20international%20disputes (last visited May 1, 2025).

9. US. Dep't of State, Archive, https://2001-2009.state.gov/r/pa/ho/time/wwii/98681.htm#:~:text=The%20Bretton%20Woods%20Conference%2C%20officially,post%2DWWII%20international%20monetary%20system (last visited May 1, 2025).

10. *Id.* As described in Chapter 3, the International Bank for Reconstruction and Development is the main organ of the World Bank. *See* Chapter 1 herein for more information regarding the formation of the IMF, as the charters for the IMF and the World Bank were drafted at the same conference.

11. United Nations, https://www.un.org/en/about-us/history-of-the-un/preparatory-years (last visited May 1, 2025). For more information regarding the formation of the United Nations, *see* Chapter 4 herein.

12. https://www.iadb.org/en/who-we-are/about-idb/history-idb. (June 26, 2023).

13. *Id.* For more information regarding the formation of the IDB, *see* Chapter 2 herein.

Privileges and Immunities

The intergovernmental organizations discussed herein have substantial privileges and immunities afforded to them pursuant to the U.S. Code.[14] The International Organizations Immunities Act (the Act) was enacted December 29, 1945 (22 U.S.C. §§ 288 *et seq*).

Congress passed the Act in anticipation of the IMF, World Bank, and United Nations setting up headquarter locations within the United States, as all of these organizations were created in 1945 after World War II seeking to "stabiliz[e] the international economy, rebuild[] war-torn nations, and maintain[] international peace and security."[15] At the time of the Act's passing, international organizations enjoyed nearly absolute immunity from suit.[16] In 2019, however, the U.S. Supreme Court held in *Budha Ismail Jam, et al. v. International Finance Corp.* that the Act is inextricably tied with the immunities enjoyed by foreign governments within the United States, which is now restricted to sovereign acts, and not commercial acts.[17] This restrictive view of the immunities started with the State Department's interpretation in 1952 and was codified by Congress in 1976.[18] However, each organization's charter may specify a different level of immunity.[19] Specifically, as it relates to those covered in this book:

14. 22 U.S.C. § 288a.

15. Budha Ismail Jam, et al. v. Int'l Fin. Corp., 139 S. Ct. 759, 586 U.S. 199 (2021) holding that the default immunities enjoyed by international organizations under the Act are tied to those enjoyed by foreign governments and evolves with those same restrictions and freedoms. The Foreign Sovereign Immunities Act passed in 1976 codifies the State Department's view that foreign sovereigns in the United States are immune only as it relates to their sovereign acts—commercial acts akin to an act in which a private person would partake are no longer immune from suit be default. The reason for this change is that "widespread and increasing practice on the part of governments of engaging in commercial activities made it necessary to enable persons doing business with them to have their rights determined in the courts." *Id.*, citing Letter from Jack B. Tate, Acting Legal Advisor, Dep't of State, to Acting Attorney General Philip B. Pearlman (May 19, 1952), reprinted in 26 Dep't State Bull. 984-985 (1952) (internal quotations omitted).

16. *Id.*

17. *Id.*

18. *Id.*

19. *Id.* at 14.

- **For the IMF:** "[T]he Fund, its property and its assets, wherever located and by whomsoever held, shall enjoy immunity from every form of judicial process except to the extent that it expressly waived its immunity for the purpose of any proceedings or by the terms of any contract."[20] In addition, the "[p]roperty and assets of the Fund, wherever located and by whomsoever held, shall be immune from search, requisition, confiscation, expropriation or any other form of seizure by executive or legislative action."[21] "The Fund, its assets, property, income, and its operations and transactions authorized by this Agreement shall be immune from all taxation and from all customs duties. The Fund shall also be immune from liability for the collection or payment of any tax or duty."[22] "No tax shall be levied on or in respect of salaries and emoluments paid by the Fund to Executive Directors, Alternates, officers, or employees of the Fund who are not local citizens, local subjects, or other local nationals."[23]
- **For the United Nations:** "The [United Nations] shall enjoy in the territory of each of its Members such legal capacity as may be necessary for the exercise of its functions and the fulfillment of its purposes."[24] And further, "1. The [United Nations] shall enjoy in the territory of each of its Members such privileges and immunities as are necessary for the fulfilment of its purposes. 2. Representatives of the Members of the United Nations and officials of the [United Nations] shall similarly enjoy such privileges and immunities as are necessary for the independent exercise of their functions in connection with the [United Nations]. 3. The General Assembly [of the United Nations] may make recommendations with a view to determining the details of the application of paragraphs 1 and 2 of

---

20. Articles of Agreement of the International Monetary Fund, Article IX, Section 3.

21. *Id.* Section 4.

22. *Id.* Section 9.

23. *Id.* Section 9(b).

24. United Nations Charter, Article 104.

this Article or may propose conventions to the Members of the United Nations for this purpose."[25]

- **For the World Bank:** "All governors, executive directors, alternates, officers and employees of the Bank (i) shall be immune from legal process with respect to acts performed by them in their official capacity except when the Bank waives this immunity; (ii) not being local nationals, shall be accorded the same immunities from immigration restrictions, alien registration requirements and national service obligations and the same facilities as regards exchange restrictions as are accorded by members to the representatives, officials and employees of comparable rank of other members; (iii) shall be granted the same treatment in respect of travelling facilities as is accorded by members to representatives, officials and employees of comparable rank of other members."[26] Further, "(a) the Bank, its assets, property, income and its operations and transactions authorized by this Agreement, shall be immune from all taxation and from all customs duties. The Bank shall also be immune from liability for the collection or payment of any tax or duty. (b) No tax shall be levied on or in respect of salaries and emoluments paid by the Bank to executive directors, alternates, officials or employees of the Bank who are not local citizens, local subjects, or other local nationals. (c) No taxation of any kind shall be levied on any obligation or security issued by the Bank (including any dividend or interest thereon) by whomsoever held; (i) which discriminates against such obligation or security solely because it is issued by the Bank; or (ii) if the sole jurisdictional basis for such taxation is the place or currency in which it is issued, made payable or paid, or the location of any office or place of business maintained by the Bank. (d) No taxation of any kind shall be levied on any obligation or security guaranteed by the Bank (including any dividend or interest thereon) by whomsoever held: (i) which discriminates against such obligation or security solely because it is

25. *Id.* Article 105.
26. IBRD Articles of Agreement, Article VII, Section 8.

guaranteed by the Bank; or (ii) if the sole jurisdictional basis for such taxation is the location of any office place of business maintained by the Bank."[27]

- **For the IDB:** "Property and assets of the bank shall, wheresoever located and by whomsoever held, be immune from all forms of seizure, attachment, or execution before the delivery of final judgment against the Bank."[28] "Property and assets of the Bank shall, wheresoever located and by whomsoever held, shall be considered public international property and shall be immune from search, requisition, confiscation, expropriation or any other form of taking or foreclosure by executive or legislative action."[29] "All governors, executive directors, alternate, officers, and employees of the Bank shall have the following privileges and immunities: (a) Immunity from legal process with respect to acts performed by them in their official capacities, except when the Bank waives this immunity. (b) When not local nationals, the same immunities from immigration restrictions, alien registration requirement and national service obligations and the same facilities as regards exchange provisions as are accorded by members to the representatives, officials, and employees of comparable rank of other members. (c) The same privileges in respect of travelling facilities as are accorded by members to representatives, officials, and employees of comparable rank of other members."[30] "(a) The Bank, its property, other assets, income, and the operations and transactions it carries our pursuant to the Agreement, shall be immune from all taxation and from all customs duties. The Bank shall also be immune from any obligation relating to the payment, withholding or collecting of any tax, or duty. (b) No tax shall be levied on or in respect of salaries and emoluments paid by the Bank to executive directors, alternates, officials or employees of the Bank who are not local citizens or other

27. IBRD Articles of Agreement, Article VII, Section 9.

28. Agreement Establishing the Inter-American Development Bank 1987, Article XI, Section 3.

29. *Id.* Section 4.

30. *Id.* Section 8.

local nationals. (c) No tax of any kind shall be levied on any obligation or security issued by the Bank, including any dividend or interest thereon, by whomsoever held: (i) which discriminates against such obligation or security solely because it is issued by the Bank; or (ii) if the sole jurisdictional basis for such taxation is the place or currency in which it is issued, made payable or paid, or the location of any office or place of business maintained by the Bank. (d) No tax of any kind shall be levied on any obligation or security guaranteed by the Bank, including any dividend or interest thereon, by whomsoever held: (i) which discriminates against such obligation or security solely because it is guaranteed by the Bank; or (ii) if the sole jurisdictional basis for such taxation is the location of any office or place of business maintained by the Bank."[31]

Generally, intergovernmental organizations have the same immunity from legal process as do foreign governments; however, these organizations can expressly waive their immunities by contract.[32] Some of those privileges are:[33]

- Sovereignty in its premises;
- Protection of the premises from intrusion, damage, disturbances of the peace or impairment of dignity by the country in which the premises is located;
- Premises as well as furnishings and property thereon as well as the means of transport to are immune from search and attachment;
- Exemption from national, regional, and local dues and taxes on the premises, except as payment for services rendered;

31. *Id.* Section 9. This is almost verbatim the language used in the World Bank's (IBRD) Articles of Agreement. This similarity is not surprising. Given that the banks have similar purposes, albeit different geographic areas of focus, it makes sense the banks should have the same privileges and immunities within their member countries.

32. 22 U.S.C. § 288a (b).

33. Vienna Convention on Diplomatic Relations, 1961, Articles 22, 23, and 34. The United States signed the treaty on June 29, 1961, and ratified it on November 13, 1972.

- On an employee level, exemption from all dues and taxes on the national, regional, and local level on income earned from employment with the organization.[34]

These privileges can allow these organizations to insulate themselves from any participation in a family legal matter. The organizations are typically very careful not to act in a manner that makes it appear as if they are waiving these privileges. For example, an organization will not allow a subpoena to be served upon its employees on the organization's property. However, the organization may have internal policies and procedures that will encourage the employee to be escorted just off the property with security to be served with the subpoena or otherwise face disciplinary actions in the workplace. Individual organization's policies are discussed more in detail in each chapter as applicable. Essentially, these organizations do not want their employees to abuse these privileges and immunities to the detriment of their families.

It may come as no shock, based on the immunities described herein, that the bank accounts and other financial accounts of these organizations are immune from garnishment/seizure under the doctrine of sovereign immunity unless such immunity is waived.[35]

Each of the organizations discussed in this book have made exceptions to these privileges and immunities to accept an order from a court within the United States that divides an employee's pension/retirement interest. Each organization's rules and regulations are discussed in depth herein. One exception that each of the organizations has in common, however, is that they accept U.S. state court orders to divide the pension benefits earned by their employees who are divorced in the United States.

---

34. This privilege is similarly codified in the U.S. Tax Code at 26 U.S.C. § 893(a).

35. Matter of L. LM v. AJJM, 69 N.Y.2d 924, 926 (1987). The New York Court of Appeals held that the trial court could not order the bank holding the funds of the UNJSPF on deposit to garnish or seize funds of the UN to pay to the participant's former spouse for child support arrears. Although this is a New York state case specific to the United Nations, the authors believe that because it is a holding based on federal and international privileges and immunities, it could be applicable to any organization with the same privileges and immunities in any state.

Employees of these organizations do not have claims for unemployment insurance benefits from the state because the organizations are immune from local taxing authorities.[36] As such, a New York Appellate Court determined that they are not covered employers for purposes of providing unemployment compensation.

Further, courts from multiple jurisdictions have held that these privileges make these organizations immune from suit for employment decisions, even if such decisions are made based on the person's race or gender, and which would otherwise be a prohibited action within the United States pursuant to Title VII of the Civil Rights Act of 1964.[37] The courts have reasoned here that employment decisions fall squarely within the organization's activities that are "essential to the fulfillment of its purposes, and thus an area to which immunity must extend."[38] Although some of these organizations have references within their charters or articles of agreement that discuss the importance of avoiding discrimination, such references are not the express waiver of immunity from Title VII which is required to allow such a suit.[39]

Disclaimer: Not All Intergovernmental Organizations Are Discussed Herein

This book covers only four of the intergovernmental organizations existing at the time of publishing, specifically, the International Monetary Fund, the Inter-American Development Bank, the World Bank, and the United Nations. There are many other intergovernmental organizations that may employ your clients or their spouses. If you

36. *Claim of Bohmova*, 667 N.Y.S.2d 857, 858, 246 A.D.2d 940 (1998). The finding in this case was specifically in reference to the United Nations, but states that because the UN "is immune from the taxing authority of this State and therefore is not required to pay unemployment insurance taxes." The authors believe it is reasonable to extrapolate this opinion to all similarly situated international organizations.

37. Boimah v. United Nations Gen. Assembly, 664 F. Supp. 69 (E.D.N.Y 1987); Tuck v. Pan American Health Org., 668 F.2d 547, 550 (D.C. Cir. 1981); Broadbent v. Org. of American States, 628 F.2d 27, 30–35 (D.C. Cir. 1980).

38. *Boimah*, 664 F. Supp at 71.

39. *Id.*

have a matter involving one of the other intergovernmental organizations you may use these organizations here to give you an idea of the types of benefits similar employers provide. However, you must look into the specific benefits provided by the organization in your matter to best protect your client's interests.

Jurisdiction and Foreign Divorce

Many books can and have been written on the issue of jurisdiction in divorce. This book will not attempt to cover that topic in detail but only give a brief, general overview of the issues as they relate to the topic of this book. This book will not attempt to cover issues related to child custody or child support and will only address jurisdiction related to division of assets.

Each discrete issue in a family law case can, will, and should have a different jurisdictional rule. This may mean you need to address different issues in different courts in different places. This may mean there are conflicts between courts in multiple jurisdictions that *might* have simultaneous jurisdiction. This may mean there are races to the courthouse, strategizing, and even manipulating. When you take on a case with a possible international component, you must be aware of what may happen. Never assume you have jurisdiction; you will need to dive deeper during your initial conversations with your client to determine all of the possible countries/states with jurisdiction and potentially consult with local attorneys to determine the jurisdictional rules that may best benefit your client. It is important to note that while most U.S. jurisdictional rules focus on domicile or residency, jurisdiction can be acquired due to location of wedding or citizenship as well.

Chapter 1

International Monetary Fund

1.1 What Is the International Monetary Fund

The Articles of Agreement of the International Monetary Fund (IMF) as adopted at the United Nations Monetary and Financial Conference at Bretton Woods, New Hampshire, on July 22, 1944, were originally accepted by 29 countries.[1] As of the date of publishing, 190 countries have ratified the Articles to become member countries of the IMF.[2] The Articles lay out the IMF's purposes, which include the promotion of international monetary cooperation to resolve international monetary problems.[3] The IMF achieves this generally through monitoring of its member economic and financial policies and the international monetary system.[4] The IMF also provides monetary resources to members in need through technical and financial assistance.[5] The most recent amendment of the Articles was adopted on December 15, 2010, and become effective on January 26, 2016.[6] In addition to the Articles, the IMF is governed internally by bylaws and rules and regulations. The IMF has employees worldwide and employees in the United States.

1. https://www.imf.org/external/pubs/ft/aa/index.htm.
2. *Id.*
3. *Id.*
4. *Id.*
5. *Id.*
6. *Id.*

1.2 Overview of International Monetary Fund Staff Retirement Plan (IMF SRP)

1.2.1 How It Works/Funding

The IMF Staff Retirement Plan (IMF SRP) is a contributory, defined-benefit pension plan established in 1948 by decision of the IMF Executive Board and amended on various occasions thereafter.[7] Participants in the IMF SRP contribute 7 percent of their pensionable gross salaries[8] to the plan each pay period.[9] The IMF also contributes to the IMF SRP, in amounts varying each year based on actuarial calculations; however, the IMF's contributions cover any amount of plan liabilities and administrative costs that are in excess of the participant contributions and any additional amounts necessary to fund payments.[10] Employees may run estimates of their benefits under various retirement scenarios through their HR Web.[11]

1.2.2 Who Is Eligible

All IMF employees on "open-ended" staff appointments are automatically enrolled in the IMF SRP effective as of the employee's first day.[12] Enrollment in the IMF SRP is optional for employees with a fixed or limited term of two years or more, part-time employees, the managing director and deputy managing directors, assistant to a managing director, executive director, alternate executive director, senior advisor to an executive director, advisor to an executive director, and Independent Evaluation Office director and fixed- and limited-term employees within the Independent Evaluation Office director's office.[13] Any other employment types, such as those with a fixed or limited term of less than two years or part-time employees, with the IMF are not eligible to participate in the IMF SRP.[14] Participating

---

7. INTERNATIONAL MONETARY FUND STAFF RETIREMENT PLAN HANDBOOK [hereinafter IMF SRP HANDBOOK].
8. *See* Terminology at Section 1.2.6 herein.
9. IMF SRP HANDBOOK, *supra* note 7, at 11.
10. *Id.*
11. *Id.* at 15.
12. *Id.* at 5, 6.
13. *Id.* at 6, 7.
14. *Id.* at 7.

employees have the option to continue their participation, even if their employment type changes to one in which enrollment is optional, or one in which it is prohibited.[15] If the initial employment type is optional, or the employment type changes to one that is optional, the employee will have 90 days from the beginning of that employment to opt in to participation.[16]

PRACTICE TIP

In the event an employee had multiple periods of employment with the IMF, it will be important to have the employee provide proof that all benefits from all periods of employment are being discussed, if marital.

1.2.3 Eligibility for Retirement

1.2.3.1 Normal Retirement Benefit and Vesting

A participant is always vested in their contributions to the IMF SRP. Participants are vested with the option to receive a pension/annuity benefit after completing three years of service. Termination of service prior to completing three years of service will result in the payment of a lump sum of benefits to be paid to the participant upon termination of service.

Eligibility for normal retirement simply requires the termination of employment on or after attaining age 62.[17] Payments will begin on the first of the month following termination of employment.[18]

The pension benefit is calculated as:

2.2 percent of the participant's highest average gross salary[19] for the first 25 years of service

plus

15. *Id.*
16. *Id.*
17. *Id.* at 12.
18. *Id.*
19. *See* Terminology at Section 1.2.6 herein.

1.8 percent of the participant's highest average gross salary for the next ten years of service.[20]

Thirty-five years is the maximum number of creditable years of service allowed, and the benefit payable cannot exceed 73 percent of the participant's highest average gross salary.[21]

PRACTICE TIP

The pension benefit is calculated as:

2.2 percent of the participant's highest average gross salary[22] for the first 25 years of service

plus

1.8 percent of the participant's highest average gross salary for the next ten years of service.[23]

1.2.3.2 Early Retirement[24]

The IMF SRP first applies the Rule of 50 to determine if a person is eligible for early retirement.

The Rule of 50 allows a participant to begin receiving benefits before attaining age 62 if (1) they are at least 55 years old, or (2) they are at least 50 years old and have at least three years of eligible service.[25] If a participant terminates their employment with the IMF prior to age 50, they can defer their benefit commencement date until age 50 or later.[26] In any circumstance, if a participant chooses to begin their pension before reaching age 62, the pension benefit payments

---

20. IMF SRP HANDBOOK, *supra* note 7, at 12.
21. *Id.*
22. *See* Terminology at Section 1.2.6 herein.
23. IMF SRP HANDBOOK, *supra* note 7, at 12.
24. There are other formulas to calculate the participant's benefit if the participant does not meet the eligibility requirements for early retirement under the Rule of 50. Such other formulas were not provided to the authors from the IMF and therefore could not be included in this book.
25. IMF SRP HANDBOOK, *supra* note 7, at 13.
26. *Id.*

will be reduced.[27] How much the benefits are reduced is determined by the years of eligible service at separation and the participant's age at the time benefit payments commence.[28]

The reduction to the benefit is calculated by either the Standard Rule or the Rule of 85. The reduction applied is the *smaller* of the two options.[29] The Standard Rule is 1/8 percent reduction for each month that the participant begins pension benefits before they are 62 years old. The Rule of 85 is a 1/8 percent reduction for each month that the participant's age (at the time pension benefits commence) *plus* years of service is less than 85.

1.2.3.3 Deferred Retirement/Mandatory Retirement

If a participant terminates their employment with the IMF prior to age 50, they can defer their benefit commencement date until age 50 or later.[30] If they seek to begin pension benefit payments between ages 50 and 55, they must have at least three years of eligible service to be eligible under the Rule of 50.[31] If they have over three years of eligible service, they may begin pension benefit payments at any time between ages 50 and 62.[32]

If participants are still active employees at the IMF at the time they reach age 62, they must begin to receive an immediate pension upon the termination of their employment with the IMF and are not allowed to defer payment of the pension benefit.[33] Anyone terminating employment with the IMF prior to age 62 must begin to receive their pension benefit payments at age 62.[34] For participants seeking to commence benefit payments prior to age 62, they must qualify under the Rule of 50 and their benefit will be reduced per the Standard Rule or Rule of 85, as described herein.[35]

---

27. *Id.*
28. *Id.*
29. *Id.* at 14.
30. *Id.* at 13.
31. *Id.* at 15.
32. *Id.*
33. *Id.*
34. *Id.*
35. *Id. See* Early Retirement for the IMF at Section 1.2.3.2 herein.

1.2.4 Disability Pension

The IMF may pay a disability pension to a participant if, before the age of 65, the participant becomes completely incapable of performing any duty that the IMF might reasonably call on that person to perform.[36] The pension becomes effective when the Pension Committee approves the application for the disability pension, so long as the participant continues to make their contributions to the IMF SRP through the date their application was approved.[37] If the participant is still receiving a salary up until their disability application is approved, then the contributions to the IMF SRP will continue automatically. If the participant stops receiving salary payments for any reason prior to the commencement of their disability pension (such as the use of all paid leave and the need to take leave without pay), the participant will need to make contributions to the IMF SRP directly.

The amount of the disability pension payable is equal to the pension payment the participant would have received had they begun normal or early retirement (for which the participant is eligible) as of the date of the disability retirement.[38] However, the payment is subject to a minimum, being the lower of (1) 50 percent of the participant's highest average gross salary at the time of disability retirement, or (2) a normal retirement pension had service continued to age 65 with no change in highest average gross salary after the date of disability retirement.[39]

A disability pension payable to the participant prior to their normal retirement date is not automatically part of the benefit divided by a court order. Thus, if the parties intend to divide the disability pension upon divorce they must state as much explicitly in any agreement and court order.[40]

---

36. IMF SRP HANDBOOK, *supra* note 7, at 16.

37. *Id.* The IMF SRP Handbook does not describe what happens in the event the participant stopped contributing to the IMF SRP prior to their application for a disability pension being approved.

38. *Id.*

39. *Id.*

40. Staff Retirement Plan of the International Monetary Fund, Guidance for the Division of Retirement Benefits at Divorce, Attachment A; Rules of the Administration Committee Under Section 11.3 of the Staff Retirement Plan, Paragraph 7.

PRACTICE TIP

The disability pension will not be divided by court order unless explicitly stated.

1.2.5 Currency of Payment

The default payment of IMF SRP benefits is the U.S. dollar.[41] A participant may elect to receive their benefit payments in a different currency if they are a national of the country whose currency they seek and they provide proof of repatriation, or provide proof that they have established and intend to maintain permanent residency in that country.[42] Such an election requires that at least 25 percent of the participant's benefit payment be made in such alternative currency.[43]

PRACTICE TIP

The IMF pension may be paid to a participant in any currency, provided certain requirements are met. The IMF pension payable to a former spouse will be paid in U.S. dollars or in such other currency as the participant initially elects to commence benefit payments. The parties may include in a direction to the IMF that the currency of the payment change with any changes made by the participant. If no such additional language is included in a direction, then the former spouse will receive their payment in the currency the participant initially elected to receive benefits in, or U.S. dollars, if no such other election was made.

The amount of the pension being paid in the alternative currency may be increased (and the amount of U.S. dollars decreased) only three times during retirement.[44] The U.S. dollar portion cannot be

---

41. IMF SRP Handbook, *supra* note 7, at 23.
42. *Id.*
43. *Id.*
44. *Id.*

increased unless the participant reestablishes permanent residency in the United States.[45] In the event of relocation to a third country, the participant may elect to receive payments in U.S. dollars and the currency of their new country of residence.[46]

The currency conversion rate to the alternative currency elected is the average of the rate for the 60 months prior to the participant's pension commencement date.[47]

1.2.6 Terminology

Administration Committee.[48] The Administration Committee is responsible for the administration of the SRP and is subject to the control and supervision of the Pension Committee. The Pension Committee appoints each of the five members of the Administration Committee and their alternates.

Divorce.[49] The IMF defines "divorce" to include legal separation. For any state that still has a formal decree for a "divorce from bed and board" in addition to an absolute divorce, it is important to know that a pension order can be entered for the IMF SRP solely upon the divorce from bed and board.

Eligible Surviving Spouse/Domestic Partner.[50] An eligible surviving spouse or domestic partner is the person who was married to, or in a registered domestic partnership with the participant at the time of the participant's death *and* who was married to or in a registered domestic partnership with the participant on the participant's last day of contributory service at the IMF.

Eligible Service.[51] The IMF SRP has five main categories of eligible service. What they all have in common, though, is that the participant made contributions to the IMF SRP during that period, or in a lump sum after the fact for a period of employment during which

45. *Id.*
46. *Id.*
47. *Id.* at 23–24.
48. *Id.* at 29.
49. *Id.* at 1.
50. *Id.* at 18.
51. *Id.* at 8.

contributions were not made. The categories are (1) periods when the participant works for the IMF and makes contributions to the IMF SRP; (2) periods of leave without pay, during which the participant made contributions to the IMF SRP; (3) periods of past eligible service that have been restored; (4) periods of past contractual employment for which the participant has purchased service credit; and (5) periods of eligible service that have been transferred from another international organization.[52]

Highest Average Gross Salary.[53] The average of gross salaries in any 36 consecutive months of eligible service producing the highest average. If the employee never had any salary decreases or breaks in service, then this will be their final 36 months of eligible service.

Investment Committee.[54] The Investment Committee is responsible for the management and investment of the Retirement Fund and is subject to the supervision and control of the Pension Committee. The Pension Committee appoints each of the nine members of the Investment Committee.

Pension Committee.[55] The Pension Committee is responsible for carrying out the provisions of the Plan. It is comprised of seven members, each with an alternate, including the managing director, four executive directors, one staff member selected by the managing director, and one staff member selected by the participants. The Pension Committee sets rules and investment policies, and must oversee the management and safekeeping of the SRP.

Pensionable Gross Salary.[56] The IMF pays salaries to employees net of tax, and those employees who have to pay national taxes can receive an additional amount called a "tax allowance," which is an approximation of the tax that will be owed. The salary plus the tax allowance

---

52. *See* Section 1.4.2 herein, describing the relationship with various other international organizations with which the IMF has an agreement to transfer eligible service.

53. IMF SRP Handbook, *supra* note 7, at 12.

54. *Id.*

55. *Id.* at 29.

56. *Id.* at 10.

is the pensionable gross equivalent of the net salary payment. The pensionable gross salary is the income figure used to calculate IMF SRP contributions.

Restoration of Eligible Service.[57] A participant may restore their prior service with the IMF if, after terminating service with the IMF, the participant again becomes a participant in the IMF SRP. A participant's prior eligible service is not automatically restored if benefits were paid out for that period. If a benefit was paid for that period, then the participant must notify the Appointment Committee within 90 days of being reappointed to an eligible position[58] *and* must repay any benefits received (with interest) within two years of the reappointment.

Tax Allowance.[59] An amount paid to active employees of the IMF to cover national taxes owed on their net salary received from the IMF during their employment. The IMF SRP does not pay an additional tax allowance for the SRP benefits, meaning the employees/retirees are responsible for paying any taxes owed on their IMF SRP benefits received.

1.2.7 Lump Sum/Commutation of Benefits

A participant entitled to receive normal or early retirement from the IMF SRP may elect to convert up to one-third of the pension to a lump-sum payment.[60] The election must be made before pension payments begin, and the payment of the lump sum is generally made within one month of the commencement of benefits on the pension.[61]

---

57. *Id.* at 8–9.

58. *See* Section 1.2.2 herein.

59. IMF SRP HANDBOOK, *supra* note 7, at 10. The approximation is based on the combined tax rates of the United States, France, and Germany, and are reviewed at a minimum of five-year intervals, but more frequently if necessary. The amount of salary increased for taxes is the net of tax salary. It does not include any additional benefits paid to the employee such as dependency allowances, education benefits, or overtime payments. *Id.*

60. *Id.* at 22.

61. *Id.*

Commuted benefits are paid in U.S. dollars (even to persons located in other countries).[62]

PRACTICE TIP

The plan participant can convert up to one-third of their pension into a lump-sum payment. Neither the court agreement, nor the spouse can limit their ability to do so.

The amount of the commuted benefit is actuarily calculated from the commuted portion of the pension based on the age of the participant as of the date pension benefits commence.[63]

Death benefits elected, such as a lump-sum payment to a beneficiary or annuity to a spouse or former spouse are not impacted by a commuted benefit because death benefits are calculated based on the pension prior to a commutation.[64]

1.2.8 Cost of Living Increases

Cost of living increases are applied to the pension on a monthly basis, effective May 1 of each year.[65] Immediate pensions will receive an initial cost of living increase effective on the first payment.[66] Deferred pensions will receive an initial cost of living increase effective in the first month following when the sum of the participant's age and years of eligible service total 50 years.[67] This initial cost of living increase is prorated based on the number of months between the pension commencement date and the number of months remaining until the end of the fiscal year.[68] The IMF may limit the cost of living increase in any year to 3 percent.[69] Cost of living increases are determined based on

62. *Id.*
63. *Id.*
64. *Id.*
65. *Id.* at 26.
66. *Id.*
67. *Id.*
68. *Id.*
69. *Id.*

the U.S. Consumer Price Index for All Urban Consumers for participants receiving their pension benefits in U.S. dollars.[70] Pensions being paid in other currencies receive cost of living increases based on the consumer price indices for such other countries as reported in the International Financial Statistics report published by the IMF.[71]

1.3 Pre-Retirement Survivor Benefit

1.3.1 Surviving Spouse/Domestic Partner Benefit

If the participant dies while still in the employ of the IMF, the participant's eligible surviving spouse or domestic partner[72] will receive a pension effective on the day following the participant's death.[73] The amount of the pension is 50 percent of the disability pension the participant would have received had they retired on disability on the date of their death.[74] However, this pension cannot be less than 30 percent of the participant's highest average gross salary. The eligible surviving spouse or domestic partner will receive this pension for the remainder of their lifetime. They do not have the option to leave any of this benefit to any beneficiary.

If the participant dies after leaving the employ of the IMF but before beginning to receive pension benefits and before attaining age 55, their eligible surviving spouse/domestic partner would receive 50 percent of the pension the participant would have been entitled to receive upon attaining age 55.[75] The eligible surviving spouse or domestic partner will receive this pension for the remainder of their lifetime. They do not have the option to leave any of this benefit to any beneficiary.

---

70. *Id.*

71. *Id.*

72. An eligible surviving spouse or domestic partner is the person who was married to, or in a registered domestic partnership with the participant at the time of the participant's death *and* who was married to or in a registered domestic partnership with the participant on the participant's last day of contributory service at the IMF. *See* Terminology at Section 1.2.6 herein.

73. IMF SRP HANDBOOK, *supra* note 7, at 18.

74. *Id.*

75. *Id.*

1.3.2 Lump-Sum Benefit

If there is no eligible surviving spouse or domestic partner, then a lump-sum payment will be made to the participant's beneficiary(ies).[76] The lump-sum benefit is calculated as the sum of the participant's accumulated pension contributions *plus* the annual amount of pensionable gross salary.[77] If the participant had at least two years of eligible service, the lump-sum death benefit is at minimum two times (2x) the participant's annual pensionable gross salary.[78]

1.3.3 Post-Retirement Survivor Benefit

1.3.3.1 Surviving Spouse/Domestic Partner Pension

The IMF SRP automatically provides a pension in the amount of 50 percent of the participant's unreduced pension benefit for the participant's eligible surviving spouse/domestic partner.[79] The benefit is effective on the day after the participant's death and continues for the life of the eligible surviving spouse/domestic partner.[80] If the participant retired on a disability pension, the eligible surviving spouse/ domestic partner would receive 50 percent of the disability pension, so long as it is not less than 30 percent of the participant's highest average gross salary, whichever is smaller.[81]

1.3.3.2 Elected Survivor Pension

Pursuant to section 4.6 of the IMF SRP, a participant may elect to provide a survivor pension to any designated individual.[82] Such designation will actuarially reduce the participant's pension benefit, based on the age difference between the participant and the designated survivor.[83]

---

76. *Id.*
77. *Id.*
78. *Id.*
79. *Id.* at 19.
80. *Id.*
81. *Id.*
82. *Id.* at 24.
83. *Id.*

Section 4.6 of the IMF SRP provides as follows:

4.6 Reduced Pensions with Pension to Survivor
(a) Any participant or retired participant may, by written notice received by the Administration Committee before his pension becomes effective, elect to convert the pension otherwise payable to him, or in the case of disability retirement, the early retirement pension to which the retired participant would otherwise have been entitled (excluding any portion of his pension commuted into a lump sum under Section 15.1) into two pensions, in accordance with one of the options named below. If such notice is received by the Administration Committee at least 30 days prior to the date his pension becomes effective, the election of the option hereunder by him shall become effective on the date his pension becomes effective. If such notice is received by the Administration Committee less than 30 days before the date his pension becomes effective, the election of the option hereunder shall become effective 30 days after the date such notice is received. The amounts of the two pensions after conversion shall be determined using the actuarial assumptions in paragraph 2 of Schedule D.

Option 1. A reduced pension payable, when effective, to him during his life, and a pension, equal in amount to such reduced pension, payable after his death during the life of, and to, the person nominated by him by written designation duly witnessed and filed with the Administration Committee when he elected the option, but only if such person survives him; or

Option 2. A reduced pension payable, when effective, to him during his life, and after his death a pension payable at one half the rate of his reduced pension during the life of, and to, the person nominated by him by written designation duly witnessed and filed with the Administration Committee when he elected the option, but only if such person survives him; or

Option 3. A reduced pension payable, when effective, to him during his life, and after his death a pension payable at such rate as he shall specify, and during the life of, and to, the person nominated by him by written designation duly witnessed and filed with the Administration Committee when he elected the option, but only if such person survives him.

(b) An election of an option may be revoked or changed by a participant or a retired participant only by written notice received by the Administration Committee before the date when his pension becomes effective, and any such change shall be treated as a revocation of the prior option and the election of a new option. If the participant or retired participant or the person designated by him dies before the date when such option becomes effective, any election of such option hereunder shall be of no effect and any benefits payable to him or on his account shall be determined and paid in all respects as if no option had been elected by him.

(c) Any retired participant who, after his contributory service has ceased, marries anyone other than the individual who had been the retired participant's domestic partner at the time he first began receiving benefits under the Plan, or enters into a domestic partnership may elect, irrevocably, by written notice filed with the Administration Committee by January 1, 1991, or within one year following such marriage or registration of such domestic partnership with the Administration Committee, if later, to reduce his own pension in accordance with this Section 4.6 and paragraph 2 of Schedule D in order to provide a survivor's pension following his death to the spouse or domestic partner, in such amount as shall be designated in the notice, subject to the limits of subsection (d) below and to the extent permitted by applicable law; provided that an election of a pension for a spouse or domestic partner under this subsection (c) shall not be effective if the retired participant dies within one year following the marriage or registration of the domestic partnership, except that the Administration Committee may, for good cause, decide to waive the latter requirement.

(d) Notwithstanding the foregoing provisions of this Section 4.6, no option may be elected thereunder that would result in either:

(i) the amount of the reduced pension payable to the retired participant being less than one half the pension that would have been payable to him if no option had been elected by him; or

(ii) the payment to the designated survivor of a pension that, together with any pension payable to such survivor pursuant to Section 4.9, would exceed the amount of the reduced pension payable to the retired participant.

Two restrictions are placed on the election of survivor pensions. First, the amount of all survivor pensions (including spouse or former spouse pensions) cannot be more than the amount of the reduced pension the participant receives.[84] Second, the reduced pension the participant receives cannot be less than half of the unreduced pension the participant would have received had the participant not elected for any survivor pensions.[85]

PRACTICE TIP

Survivor pension restrictions:

1. ***Amount of all survivor pensions paid must be less than the reduced pension received by the participant; and***
2. ***Participant's pension cannot be reduced by more than 50 percent.***

An election for a survivor pension is irrevocable once it becomes effective, even if the designated beneficiary dies first.[86] The beneficiary designation becomes effective once it reduces a pension payment

84. *Id.*
85. *Id.*
86. *Id.* at 25.

made to the participant.[87] The latest a beneficiary designation can be made is 30 days prior to the pension payments commencing.[88]

A participant may add a beneficiary after they have begun to receive pension benefits in limited circumstances. Specifically, if a participant gets married or establishes a domestic partner relationship during retirement, they may elect to provide that person with a survivor benefit.[89] The election must be made within one year of the date of marriage, and the election becomes effective in the 13th month following the date of marriage.[90] Once effective, the election is irrevocable.[91] Such election will reduce the participant's pension payments actuarily based on the age difference between the participant and the new survivor and the amount of the benefit provided.[92]

Notably, if a former spouse is to receive a survivor benefit, this is the benefit they would receive. It must be secured by the participant executing a designation form and cannot be secured via a court order. Such a designation remains in place after divorce. So, if representing the participant and the designation is still revocable, it is important to advise them to file a new designation if the intent is not to provide such benefit to the former spouse.

PRACTICE TIP

A former spouse survivor benefit cannot be secured via court order and must be designated via the IMF's designation form.

1.3.3.3 Lump-Sum Death Benefit

If there is no eligible surviving spouse/domestic partner, the IMF SRP will pay benefits in accordance with the beneficiary designation on file.[93] The lump-sum is calculated as the excess of any remaining

87. *Id.* at 24.
88. *Id.*
89. *Id.* at 25.
90. *Id.*
91. *Id.*
92. *Id.*
93. *Id.* at 20.

participant contributions (if any) with interest thereon (after deducting the pension benefit payments made, including any commutations) *plus* a percent of the annual, unreduced pension the participant would have received.[94] The applicable percent of the participant's annual, unreduced pension is 200 percent if death is before age 65, and decreases by 20 percent each year until reaching a minimum of 50 percent at age 73 or older for the participant's death.[95]

1.3.3.4 Children's Benefits

If the participant, at the time of their death, has unmarried children, the IMF SRP will pay benefits to the children (up to a maximum of three children's benefits, even if there are more than three children) so long as the children are unmarried, up to the age of 19 years old (or 22 years old if full-time students), or for so long as a child is incapacitated, if the incapacity started before the age of 19.[96] The children must have been born prior to or within ten months of the participant's death.[97]

Payments to minors are made to the surviving spouse/domestic partner or legal guardian of the minor.[98] When the eligible child has a living parent, the annual benefit payment is equal to one-third of the annual pension that the participant would have been eligible to receive upon their death.[99] If the eligible child does not have a living parent, then the annual benefit is equal to one-quarter of the annual pension that the participant would have been eligible to receive upon their death.[100] Benefit payments are made on a monthly basis, and are adjusted for cost-of-living increases effective May 1 of each year.[101]

94. *Id.*
95. *Id.*
96. *Id.*
97. *Id.*
98. *Id.*
99. *Id.*
100. *Id.*
101. *Id.*

1.4 Withdrawals and Transfers to Other Institutions

1.4.1 Withdrawal Benefit

A withdrawal benefit is a one-time payment that terminates the participant's eligibility to receive any other benefits under the IMF SRP after taking the withdrawal benefit. It is calculated as 20 percent (of the participant's highest average gross salary for each of the first ten years of eligible service, with a maximum of 200 percent of the highest average gross salary).[102] This benefit is paid in only U.S. dollars.[103]

Participants are required to withdraw their benefits in the IMF SRP if they terminate employment with the IMF prior to age 50 and with fewer than three years of eligible service.[104] Participants have the option to take a withdrawal benefit if they terminate employment with the IMF before age 50 with more than three years of eligible service, after age 50 with three to five years of eligible service, or after age 55 with less than five years of eligible service.[105] It seems that in any other situation, the participant must receive either a deferred or immediate pension benefit.[106]

Participants who elect a deferred retirement benefit upon termination of service may, if eligible, change their mind at any time prior to beginning to receive the deferred benefit, and may elect to receive the withdrawal benefit instead.[107]

---

102. *Id.* at 17.
103. *Id.*
104. *Id.* at 16.
105. *Id.* at 17.
106. The author notes here that these rules do not quite make sense. For example, a person leaving the employ of the IMF at age 51 with two years of service would not have the option to receive a withdrawal benefit, but if they remained employed for another year, to have three years of eligible service and be age 52, they would have such an option.
107. IMF SRP HANDBOOK, *supra* note 7, at 17.

1.4.2 Transfers to Other Institutions

The IMF has agreements with the Asian Development Bank, the United Nations, the Inter-American Development Bank, and the World Bank Group to transfer employees' interest in the respective pension systems.[108] A participant in the IMF SRP can transfer their interest in the IMF SRP to the retirement system of the Asian Development Bank, United Nations, Inter-American Development Bank, or the World Bank Group upon becoming employed with one of those organizations if they meet the requirements for the specific agreements between the IMF and each institution.[109] Each agreement to transfer the interest between the organizations' retirement systems is specific to those two institutions. Some may have determined their systems and the position(s) held by the participant are similar enough that the transfer is on a one-to-one basis. Other agreements recognize a difference in the plans and compensation for the participant's employment that requires the transfer to be on a basis other than one-to-one. In such circumstances, it is important to have a call with the retirement system office for the plan that will be divided to understand how the participant in your case is impacted. For example, it may require an adjustment to the marital share formula to ensure that the benefit is being divided as the parties intend.

PRACTICE TIP

Not all transfers between institutions are on a one-to-one basis. If your case involves a transfer, be sure to communicate with the retirement office for the plan that will be divided to ensure that their implementation of the division language is what the parties intend.

108. Only the transfer agreement with the United Nations Joint Staff Retirement Plan is available to the public.

109. Not all agreements between the institutions are available, so only those available are described herein.

1.4.2.1 IMF SRP and the United Nations

The agreement with the United Nations Joint Staff Pension Fund (UNJSPF) provides that a former participant in the UNJSPF who has not otherwise received their benefit from the UNJSPF, and who becomes a participant in the IMF SRP within six months of the termination of their participation in the UNJSPF and who opts to transfer their interest in the UNJSPF within 30 days of commencing their participation in the IMF SRP, may transfer such interest.[110] The interest shall be transferred on a one-to-one basis, such that the contributions plus interest thereon that the participant made in the UNJSPF shall be transferred dollar-for-dollar, the amount of time served in the UNJSPF shall be transferred, and the remuneration received at the UNJSPF shall be recorded as the participant's remuneration for the period of service in the UNJSPF.[111] Similarly, any participant in IMF SRP who seeks to transfer their interest to the UNJSPF due to new employment with the United Nations can do so if they meet the aforementioned criteria.[112] The amount of benefit transferred will be the same as a transfer from the UNJFPS to the IMF SRP.[113]

1.5 Division in Divorce

A participant's IMF SRP can be divided to provide payments for marital property division, or the payment of alimony (spousal support) and/or child support. The amount of the participant's pension that can be redirected to a former spouse for alimony or marital property purposes is 50 percent of the benefit attributable to the eligible service during the marriage.[114] If payments from the pension are being made for child support purposes, then the maximum amount that

---

110. Agreement between the United Nations Joint Staff Pension Board and the International Monetary Fund on the continuity and transfer of pension rights and participants in the United Nations Joint Staff Pension Fund and of participants in the Staff Retirement Plan of the International Monetary Fund. Article 2. December 20, 1979.

111. *Id.*

112. *Id.* Article 3.

113. *Id.*

114. IMF SRP HANDBOOK, *supra* note 7, at 26.

can be paid to the former spouse is 66 2/3 percent of the participant's pension payments.[115]

In order for payments to be made from the IMF SRP for child support purposes, the participant must already be receiving benefit payments from the IMF SRP. Meaning, the participant must already be retired from the IMF and receiving the IMF SRP pension payments in order for the IMF SRP to accept and implement an order requiring payments of child support to a former spouse.

PRACTICE TIP

Be aware of the cap on the allowed pension benefits that can be distributed to the former spouse. The cap is 50 percent if only for alimony and or property division, or 66 2/3 percent if the amount includes child support.

Payments are made from the IMF SRP pursuant to court orders prospectively only.[116] This means that in a case where the IMF employee is already retired, or will be retired before the court order is submitted to and accepted by the IMF, the parties should discuss whether a direct payment scheme from the participant to the former spouse should be included in the settlement agreement. Since the plan only pays the former spouse after the order is accepted, this leaves a possibility that the retired participant could be receiving benefits from the plan while the former spouse is not.

As it relates to child support and alimony, it means that the plan will not make payments to settle arrears owed to the former spouse. The SRP will only make payments for the continuing obligation, and not any missed payments that should have been made directly from the participant to the former spouse.

---

115. *Id.*
116. *Id.*

PRACTICE TIP

Requests for divorce related information should be made to:

International Monetary Fund
Attn: SRP Team
700 19th Street, N.W.
Washington DC 20431
Email: SRP@IMF.org

1.5.1 How to Divide the IMF SRP

The IMF pension requires a direction by the participant, or request by the former spouse, in addition to the court order or clear settlement agreement language that is incorporated into a divorce decree. Note, the plan will not make any retroactive payments to the former spouse, all payments are prospective either from the effective (future) date stated or the first day of the month at least 60 days after the IMF receives the court order and necessary additional documents.[117]

For a divorce in which the participant is already receiving the benefits from the IMF plan, the attorneys should take care to address how the funds will be divided before the court order is received and accepted by the IMF. For example, the participant could pay the former spouse their share directly on a monthly basis. Since such payments will be taxed at the participant's tax rate prior to the court order being effective, the parties should also address in any agreement whether the payments to the former spouse will be net of tax, or if the former spouse will reimburse the participant for any tax paid on the former spouse's share. Sample language for this is included in Chapter 7 herein. Note, the tax allowance is not applicable here because the tax allowance is only to cover national taxes for the employee's salary and *not* for the employee's pension benefit.

117. Retirement Plan of the International Monetary Fund. *Guidance for the Division of Retirement Benefits at Divorce.* Attachment A, Paragraph 9.

PRACTICE TIP

The tax allowance is not applicable in the division of the IMP SRP because the tax allowance is only for the employee's salary, not their pension benefit.

1.5.2 How to Divide the Survivor Benefit

As described by in Section 1.3 herein, the pre-retirement survivor benefit is payable to an eligible surviving spouse/domestic partner or designated beneficiaries. Therefore, if the former spouse seeks a portion of this benefit, they must be designated as a beneficiary on the IMF SRP form. However, if the participant remarries prior to terminating employment with the IMF and remains married to that person through the participant's death, then the new spouse will receive the full pre-retirement survivor benefit and the former spouse will not receive a benefit. Considering this information, this benefit may not be worth much energy in negotiation since it can so easily be taken away from the former spouse. Conversely, it might be easy for the participant to agree to, since it does not impact the benefit to a new spouse, should the participant remarry.

In the event the parties agree that the former spouse should receive a share of the lump-sum death benefit (in the event the participant does not remarry) then the designation to the former spouse can be included in the court order. However, it must be drafted such that the order requires the participant to file the beneficiary designation for the former spouse. The IMF can only implement a beneficiary designation that is made via their appropriate forms; it cannot be secured only by including it in the court order.

PRACTICE TIP

Be aware of the effect of remarriage on the survivor benefit awarded to the former spouse. Consider life insurance as an alternative.

The reason the order is not sufficient to secure the benefit is because the IMF is not a party to the divorce case and not subject to a state court's order. Therefore, it will not abide by a provision in a court order to provide a survivor benefit to a former spouse.

As for the post-retirement survivor benefit, the requirement is the same as the pre-retirement death benefit that if it is included in the court order then it must be phrased such that it is the participant's requirement to elect the former spouse to receive the benefit through the proper forms. If the participant does not timely file the requisite forms with the IMF, then the survivor benefit for the former spouse is not secured. The form must be submitted to the IMF at least 30 days prior to the participant's commencement of benefits from the IMF SRP. Once the participant commences benefits, the election of the former spouse to receive the benefit is irrevocable. This is true even if the former spouse dies first. Meaning that the reduction to provide the survivor benefit will continue for the lifetime of the participant, even if the former spouse dies first and therefore is not alive to receive a survivor benefit.[118] The spouse survivor benefit exists separate from the optional post-retirement survivor benefit that is available for a former spouse, so if the former spouse is properly elected, the remarriage of the participant will not impact the former spouse's post-retirement survivor benefits.

1.5.3 How to Allocate the Cost of Survivor Benefit

The "cost" of the survivor benefit cannot be easily shifted per se, as the "cost" is a reduction in the pension "off the top." The participant may be able to obtain estimates from the IMF SRP of the pension benefit, as well as the reduction for the intended survivor benefit election. The amount of the reduction is calculated based on the age of each party as of the participant's benefit commencement date and thus cannot be estimated by counsel. Obtaining such information will allow the parties to decrease the amount of the former spouse's share of the pension during the participant's lifetime to account for the "cost" to provide the survivor benefit. Alternatively, the parties can stipulate in the agreement and order if the "cost" will be shifted

---

118. IMF SRP Handbook, *supra* note 7, at 24–25.

at all. If so, it must be phrased to give the IMF permission to adjust the marital share fraction to reduce the award to the former spouse to effectively shift this "cost."

Since the IMF will not implement a survivor benefit pursuant to a court order, any language in the order allowing a change in the award to the former spouse to account for the cost of the survivor benefit will only be effective if the participant timely files the designation form.

1.5.4 Treatment of Post-Divorce Salary Adjustments

The parties can specify in the court order that the former spouse's payment be calculated excluding any increases in the participant's salary that are due to increases in the participant's salary after the date of divorce (or other specified date). If there is nothing in the order addressing a limit on the inclusion of post-divorce salary adjustments in the calculation of the former spouse's share, then the IMF will apply the former spouse's share to the participant's final pension amount. Some states have statutes or case law to determine how that state will treat post-divorce salary adjustments.[119]

1.5.5 Cost of Living Adjustments

The parties may include in the court order to award the former spouse with cost-of-living adjustments pursuant to the IMF SRP Articles. If it is not included in the court order, the former spouse will not receive the cost-of-living adjustments.

---

119. *See* 23 Pa. Cons. Stat. § 3501(a) (property acquired after separation excluded from marital property); Gordon v. Gordon, 545 Pa. 391, 681 A.2d 732 (1996) (salary to be used to determine marital portion of pension is as of divorce, not retirement; but spouse may be entitled to higher benefit resulting from change in plan after divorce); Armstrong v. Armstrong, 34 S.W.3d 83 (Ky. 2000) (post-divorce increased earnings and resulting pension benefits are separate property of employee-spouse); Rivera-Santos v. Rivera-Santos, 862 So. 2d 480 (La. 2003) (former spouse share of pension based on amount of pension payable at retirement, but employee may seek exception if meets three-part test, including proof that increase resulting from his/her post-divorce individual efforts); Hicks v. Hicks, 348 S.W.3d 281, 287 (Tex. App. 2011) (high 36-month average should be calculated as of the date of divorce, rather than the date of retirement).

PRACTICE TIP

The plan participant can convert up to one-third of their pension into a lump-sum payment. Neither the court, agreement, nor the spouse can limit their ability to do so.

1.5.6 Orders

The IMF will accept a court order or the parties' agreement in addition to a direction from the participant or request from the alternate payee/former spouse.[120] We strongly believe it is best practice to draft a separate court order regarding the division of the IMF pension, or any retirement division for that matter. The reason is to have one straightforward and self-contained document devoted to this one important asset. It is easy for agreements to get complicated and for the division of a single asset to be the result of negotiation and many compromises that may be described within the agreement. The plan does not need to know, nor do they want to know, the reason the division is the way it is. The plan only wants to know that the division is what was agreed to/ordered by the court, and that the agreed upon division is permissible within the plan rules. Most plans, including all of the plans described in this book, will not interpret an agreement or court order if it is vague. Therefore, if there is vague or complicated language, the documents will very likely be rejected. However, if there is a court order that clearly states the intended division, the odds of acceptance are much higher.

The IMF must receive both a direction from the participant describing the division of benefits and the underlying court order or agreement between the parties.[121] This requirement is so that the IMF has secondary documentation that the division being directed by the participant or requested by the former spouse is what was ordered or agreed upon. The IMF will review the court order for conformity to

120. Retirement Plan of the International Monetary Fund. *Guidance for the Division of Retirement Benefits at Divorce.* Attachment A, Paragraph 9.

121. *Id.* at 2.

the plan rules and regulations but will not otherwise review or opine on the merits of the order.[122]

While the IMF does have a model court order for attorneys to use, its use is not required. The IMF will accept any "judgment, decree, qualified domestic relations order (QDRO), or court-approved settlement agreement arising from a divorce or separation proceeding."[123]

The order may be for the division of property, child support payments, or alimony payments.[124] Also, the order must create or recognize the alternate payee/former spouse's right "to receive a portion of benefits with respect to a participant" from the plan.[125]

The IMF must also receive a direction from the participant or a request from the alternate payee/former spouse. The direction must state the name of the participant, that the direction is made pursuant to section 11.3 of the Staff Retirement Plan, that the participant irrevocably directs the plan to make payments to their former spouse, that the amount paid to the former spouse is attributable to pensionable service during the marriage, and that the benefits being provided to the former spouse do not exceed 50 percent of the amount earned during the marriage.[126] The participant has 30 business days to submit the direction to the IMF.[127]

PRACTICE TIP

Cost of living adjustments must be explicitly divided for the former spouse to receive them.

In the event the participant does not submit a direction timely, the former spouse may submit a request to the IMF.[128] The former spouse's request shall include the same information as required in the

122. Staff Retirement Plan of the International Monetary Fund, *Guidance for the Division of Retirement Benefits at Divorce*, Section IV.A.

123. *Id.* Section II.B.

124. *Id.*

125. *Id.*

126. *Id.* at 13.

127. *Id.* at 2.

128. *Id.* at 2, 23.

direction, as well as a certification that at least 30 business days have passed since the entry of the court order and to the best of the former spouse's knowledge the participant has not submitted a direction.[129]

If the court order is submitted to the IMF with a request from the former spouse rather than a direction from the participant, the IMF will notify both parties but the participant will be notified of their right to consent or object to the request within 30 business days.[130] If the participant objects to the request, the Administration Committee (the Committee) will review the objection within 45 business days. If either party wants to object to the Committee's acceptance of a direction or request, they must do so within 90 business days of the Committee's decision by requesting review of the decision by the Committee.[131]

If the Committee is satisfied that there is a true dispute, they can direct that any payments that are supposed to be made to the former spouse be directed to an interest-bearing account at the Bank-Fund Staff Federal Credit Union while the dispute is being resolved.[132]

Once the Committee is satisfied that the court order is correct and neither party makes further objections, it will make a note in the participant's record of the court order if the benefit is not yet payable.[133] Once the IMF knows when the benefit will become payable, they will notify the former spouse and direct the former spouse to fill out forms in advance of the payment date.[134]

1.5.7 Additional Forms

If the parties agree that the former spouse will receive a survivor benefit of any kind, they must make sure the participant fills out and submits the Designated Beneficiary Form. It is beneficial to the former spouse if the agreement or court order provides that the former spouse may ask for proof of their continued beneficiary or survivor designation status. If not, they might not be able to check and ensure the participant is continuing to maintain such designation.

---

129. *Id.* at 23.
130. *Id.* Section III.B.
131. *Id.* Section IV.B.
132. *Id.*
133. *Id.* Section V.A.
134. *Id.* Section V.B.

1.5.8 Contact Information

Court orders dividing the retirement benefit are processed by the Staff Retirement Plan Team at the IMF:

International Monetary Fund
Staff Retirement Plan Team
700 19th Street, N.W.
Washington, DC 20431
SRP@IMF.org

That is the address to send any final, certified copies of court orders, judgments of divorce, and section 11.3 directives.

Draft orders can be submitted to the SRP Team at SRP@imf.org for review and preliminary approval before the order is signed by the parties and submitted to the court.

1.6 Remarriage of Employee

If the employee remarries during their retirement, they have one year following the date of marriage to elect to provide a survivor pension to the new spouse, and it will become effective in the 13th month following the marriage.[135] Once the election is effective, it is irrevocable, even if the new spouse dies before the employee.[136]

1.7 Remarriage of Alternate Payee

Remarriage of the alternate payee does not impact payments from the IMF SRP.

1.8 Appeals

The Administration Committee's final decisions may be appealed to the IMF Administrative Tribunal after all other administrative remedies have been exhausted, including seeing a reconsideration by the Administration Committee pursuant to the Rules of Procedure.[137] Many of the IMF Administrative Tribunal's opinions can be

135. IMF SRP HANDBOOK, *supra* note 7, at 25.
136. *Id.*
137. *Id.* at 30.

found online on the IMF website. The petitioner may request an oral proceeding, in accordance with Rule XIII, and provide exhibits, witnesses, and testimony, including that of experts. The petitioner may be represented by counsel.

1.9 Other Benefits

1.9.1 Benefits for Families Stationed Overseas

IMF employees who are not from the United States receive certain travel benefits. Specifically, staff may be eligible for support to visit home with dependents.[138] The IMF Human Resources Department also provides an abundance of support including career services for spouses of employees, education and schooling options for non-U.S. citizens, English courses, and legal resources.[139] Spouses of IMF employees should reach out to the IMF HR Department directly for additional information.

1.9.2 College Tuition and Expenses

The IMF provides some educational benefits for certain children of IMF employees.[140] These benefits may include tuition assistance, room and board contributions, and contributions to travel, based on various factors. While these benefits cannot be divided in divorce nor secured by an agreement between the parents,[141] they can be substantial financial assistance to the parents. Therefore, the benefits that the child or family may be eligible for should be obtained during negotiations so that any necessary steps to secure the benefits can be taken. Questions should be directed to the IMF HR Department for additional information.

---

138. Int'l Monetary Fund, Compensation and Benefits (2025), https://www.imf.org/en/About/Recruitment/life-at-the-imf/compensation-and-benefits.

139. *Id.*

140. *Id.*

141. These benefits are regulated by IMF rules and require the employee and/or family to satisfy certain requirements to qualify for the benefit. Therefore, while the parties cannot guarantee they will receive such benefits and secure them via their agreement, they can agree to act in ways that will tend to make them eligible for such benefits, or not jeopardize their eligibility in the future.

1.9.3 Other Benefits

The IMF provides multiple other benefits to its employees and their families, such as health insurance benefits (and continuation thereof for a child of the marriage after the divorce) and life insurance coverage. The information is not made public and must be requested in each case to ensure the correct information is being obtained. Questions and requests for information should be directed to the IMF HR Department.

Chapter 2

Inter-American Development Bank

The Inter-American Development Bank (IDB or the Bank) was established in 1959 to provide financial and technical support to national and sub-national governments in Latin America and the Caribbean.[1] The IDB consists of three entities, specifically, the IDB that works in the public sector; IDB Invest, which works in the private sector; and IDB Law, which researches innovative methods to create more inclusive growth in the region.[2] The IDB consists of 48 member countries, including the United States as a non-borrowing country, meaning that the United States only provides funding for the IDB but does not receive funds or loans from the IDB.[3] In order to be a member in the IDB, local countries must also be a member of the Organization of American States, and nonlocal countries must be members of the IMF.[4]

2.1 Overview of Inter-American Development Bank Pension (IDB Pension)

2.1.1 How It Works/Funding

Employees of the IDB participate in the IDB Pension. Both participants and the IDB contribute to the plan on a regular basis.[5]

1. Inter-American Development Bank, https://www.iadb.org/en/who-we-are/about-idb (last visited May 1, 2025).

2. *Id.*

3. IDB, https://www.iadb.org/en/who-we-are/how-we-are-organized (last visited May 1, 2025).

4. *Id.*

5. Staff Retirement Plan, Inter-American Development Bank (2015), Section 6.1.

Participants currently contribute 10 percent of their remuneration[6] each pay period to the plan.[7] This contribution amount has been constant since January 1, 1981.[8] Prior to January 1, 1981, participants contributed less per pay period.[9] This plan is different from other pension plans in this regard in that other plans determine a participant's contribution rate as of the participant's date of hire. The IDB has determined the contribution rate to be the same for all participants, regardless of hire date.

The Bank[10] also makes two contributions.[11] The first is a percent of the total participant contributions, which the Pension Committee[12] determines to be sufficient to cover the costs of the plan.[13] This is called the "normal contribution" and it is made periodically throughout the year as determined by the Pension Committee.[14] The second contribution is the "accrued liability contribution," which is any additional amount necessary to cover all benefits of the plan not otherwise covered.[15] It is paid on a schedule as deemed necessary by the Pension Committee.[16]

The Bank is also explicitly responsible for all administrative costs of the plan.[17] This provision means that the Bank does not pass on any of the plan's administrative expenses to the participants.

2.1.2 Who Is Eligible

Every IDB employee is a participant in the plan as of their first day of service.[18] Certain employees[19] have the option not to participate

6. *See* Terminology, Section 2.1.6 herein.
7. *Id.*
8. *Id.*
9. *Id.*
10. *Id.*
11. Staff Retirement Plan, *supra* note 5, Section 6.2(a).
12. *See* Terminology, Section 2.1.6 herein.
13. *Id.*
14. *Id.*
15. *Id.*
16. *Id.*
17. Staff Retirement Plan, *supra* note 5, Section 6.2(d).
18. *Id.* Section 2.1.
19. The president, vice presidents, general manager of the corporation, executive directors of the bank, alternate executive directors of the bank, director of the

in the plan. If they wish to opt out, they must file a written notice with the executive secretary within three months of beginning their employment.[20] If representing one of these employees or their spouse, it will be important to confirm if such an election was made. If it was, then any contributions the employee made between their first date of service and the election being processed will be returned to the employee such that the employee will have no interest in the plan, and there will be no benefit to divide.[21]

2.1.3 Eligibility for Retirement

Participants who accrue less than five years of service as of their termination date are required to withdraw their interest in the plan at the time they terminate employment. By withdrawing their interest, they will not be eligible for any future payment or benefit from the plan.[22] The withdrawal benefit is calculated as:[23]

10 percent of the participant's highest average remuneration[24] *times* number of years of eligible service

plus

1 percent of the participant's highest average remuneration *times* number of years of eligible service

If such an employee (former participant) returns to the employment of the IDB, the previous service and salary associated with the withdrawn benefit will be disregarded such that any participation in the plan due to a second period of employment will be calculated as if the second employment is the only employment with the IDB.[25]

Evaluation Office, staff of the Offices of the Executive Directors (as appointed), and any appointed, part-time employee, has the option not to participate in the plan. Staff Retirement Plan, *supra* note 5, Section 2.1(b).

20. *Id.*
21. *Id.*
22. *Id.* Section 4.10(a).
23. *Id.*
24. *See* Terminology, Section 2.1.6 herein.
25. Staff Retirement Plan, *supra* note 5, Section 4.10(a).

PRACTICE TIP

A participant's withdrawal benefit at the end of fewer than five years of service is calculated as:

10 percent of the participant's highest average remuneration[26] times ***number of years of eligible service***

plus

1 percent of the participant's highest average remuneration times ***number of years of eligible service***

2.1.3.1 Participants with a Hire Date on or After January 1, 2015

2.1.3.1.1 Normal Retirement—Withdrawal Benefit Calculation

If a participant with five or more years of eligible service elects to receive a withdrawal benefit in lieu of a pension and any other benefits from the plan, such election must be made at any time before the pension becomes effective, which is at either the participant's early or normal retirement date.[27]

Participants with five or more but less than ten years of eligible service may elect either the withdrawal benefit or may receive a deferred pension, which will become effective on the participant's normal retirement date.[28]

If electing the withdrawal benefit, it is calculated as:[29]

10 percent of the participant's highest average remuneration *times* the participant's years of eligible service

plus

70 percent of the participant's highest remuneration

plus

24 percent for each year of eligible service in excess of five years

---

26. *See* Terminology, Section 2.1.6 herein.
27. Staff Retirement Plan, *supra* note 5, Section 4.4(b), (c).
28. *Id.* Section 4.4(a)(1).
29. *Id.* Section 4.10(c).

If electing to receive the pension benefit, the participant will begin to receive benefits at the participant's normal retirement age. The annual pension benefit is calculated as follows:[30]

2.5 percent of the participant's highest average remuneration

times

the number of years of eligible service

This benefit cannot be less than $50 *times* the participant's number of years of eligible service and shall not be greater than 80 percent of the participant's highest average remuneration.[31]

Participants with ten years or more eligible service may also elect to receive a withdrawal benefit in lieu of a pension and any other benefits from the plan.[32] They may also elect to receive their pension payments on or before their normal retirement date.[33]

If electing the withdrawal benefit, it is calculated as follows: [34]

10 percent of the participant's highest average remuneration
times the number of years of eligible service

plus

1 percent of the participant's highest average
remuneration for each year of eligible service

plus

180 percent of the participant's highest average remuneration
at the end of the participant's first ten years of eligible service

PRACTICE TIP

The withdrawal benefit is calculated differently based on how long the participant worked for the IDB. A court order or agreement cannot compel a participant to elect either a withdrawal benefit or a pension benefit.

30. *Id.* Section 4.1(a).
31. *Id.* Section 4.1(a) & (b).
32. *Id.* Section 4.10(c)(2).
33. *Id.* Section 4.4(a)(2).
34. *Id.* Section 4.10(c)(2).

2.1.3.1.2 Normal Retirement—Pension Benefit

If electing the pension benefit to begin at the participant's normal retirement date, the annual pension benefit is calculated as follows: [35]

2.5 percent of the participant's highest average remuneration *times* the number of years of eligible service up to and including 20 years of eligible service

plus

2 percent of the participant's highest average remuneration multiplied by the number of years between the 21st and 35th years of service

The same minimum and maximum benefit requirements for participants having fewer than ten years of eligible service apply.[36]

PRACTICE TIP

A participant's pension benefit commencing on their normal retirement date is calculated as follows:

2.5 percent of the participant's highest average remuneration times ***the number of years of eligible service up to and including 20 years of eligible service***

plus

2 percent of the participant's highest average remuneration multiplied by the number of years between the 21st and 35th years of service

2.1.3.1.3 Early Retirement

The date of early retirement eligibility and withdrawal benefits is partially dependent on the date of hire as set forth in the following sections. A participant must have at least five years of eligible service to receive an early retirement pension benefit. If electing the pension

35. *Id.* Section 4.1(a).
36. *Id.* Section 4.1(a) & (b).

benefit under an early retirement scheme, the participant must be at least 55 years old when the benefit commences.[37] The amount of the early retirement benefit is calculated as the larger of the following two calculations:

First, the benefit could be calculated solely based solely on the participant's age at commencement of the benefit. If using this calculation, they may receive a reduced benefit according to the following table:[38]

Age at Benefit Commencement[39]	Percent of Pension Received
65	100%
64	97%
63	94%
62	91%
61	87%
60	83%
59	79%
58	75%
57	70%
56	65%
55	60%

Alternatively, the benefit could be calculated based on the participant's age and length of service, combined. Under this calculation, if the participant's age at the time of termination of employment *plus* qualifying time of service, both calculated in months, equals 1,080 months, then the participant's benefit shall not be reduced.[40] If the participant's age and eligible service calculated in months is less than

37. *Id.* Section 4.2.
38. *Id.* Section 4.2(a).
39. Years are counted as full years only and are not prorated. *Id.*
40. *Id.* Section 4.2(b).

1,080, then the participant will receive a reduced benefit according to the following table:[41]

Age Plus Service (in Months)	Percent of Pension Received
1,080	100%
1,056	97%
1,032	94%
1,008	91%
984	87%
960	83%
936	79%
912	75%
888	70%
864	65%
840	60%

2.1.3.2 *Participants with a Hire Date on or After October 1, 2011, but on or Before December 31, 2014*

A participant with less than three years of eligible service who terminates employment before their normal retirement date shall be paid a withdrawal benefit calculated as follows:[42]

10 percent of the participant's highest average remuneration
times the number of years of eligible service

plus

4 percent of their highest average remuneration
for each year of eligible service

41. *Id.*
42. *Id.* Appendix VII.

PRACTICE TIP

A participant with fewer than three years of eligible service with the IDB terminating their employment before their normal retirement date is required to receive a withdrawal benefit and will not receive any further benefits from the plan.

A participant with at least three but less than five years of eligible service shall be paid a withdrawal benefit at the time of their termination of employment in the amount that is calculated as follows:[43]

10 percent of their highest average remuneration
times their years of service

plus

12 percent of their highest average remuneration

plus

30 percent of their highest average remuneration for
each year of service in excess of three years

A participant with at least five years of service and up to eight years of service may receive their benefit in the form of pension payments at their normal retirement date or can receive a withdrawal benefit as of the date they terminate employment with the IDB.[44] If they elect a withdrawal benefit, it is calculated as:[45]

10 percent of their highest average remuneration
multiplied by their number of years of service

plus

12 percent of their highest average remuneration

plus

30 percent of their highest average remuneration for
each year of service in excess of three years

---

43. *Id.*
44. *Id.*
45. *Id.*

PRACTICE TIP

A participant with three to eight years or more of eligible service with the IDB can defer their benefit and receive it in the form of a pension, or they can receive an immediate withdrawal benefit.

A participant with more than eight years of service could also elect a withdrawal benefit in lieu of pension benefits at their normal retirement date.[46] Their withdrawal benefit is calculated as:[47]

10 percent of their highest average remuneration multiplied by the number of years of service

plus

162 percent of their highest average remuneration at the end of the first eight years of service

2.1.3.2.1 Early Retirement for Participants Hired Between October 1, 2011, and December 30, 2014

A participant that has at least 15 years of qualifying service and attained 50 years of age, or at least ten years of qualifying service and attained 55 years of age before they reach their normal retirement date is eligible for early retirement.[48] If they decide to begin the pension benefits early, the benefit is calculated as a percent of their pension had they waited to retire at their normal retirement age, pursuant to the following table:[49]

Age (years)	Percent of Pension Received
65	100%
64	97%
63	94%
62	91%

46. *Id.*
47. *Id.*
48. *Id.*
49. *Id.*

Age (years)	Percent of Pension Received
61	87%
60	83%
59	79%
58	75%
57	70%
56	65%
55	60%
54	55%
53	50%
52	45%
51	40%
50	35%

Alternatively, if the participant's age at the time of termination of employment and qualifying time of service, both calculated in months, equals 1,080 months, then the participant's benefit shall not be reduced.[50] If the participant's age and eligible service calculated in months is less than 1,080, then the participant will receive a reduced benefit according to the following table:[51]

Age Plus Service (in Months)	Percent of Pension Received
1,080	100%
1,056	97%
1,032	94%
1,008	91%
984	87%
960	83%

50. *Id.*
51. *Id.*

Age Plus Service (in Months)	Percent of Pension Received
936	79%
912	75%
888	70%
864	65%
840	60%

2.1.3.3 Employees with a Hire Date on or Before September 30, 2011—Normal Benefit Calculation

Participants hired on or before September 30, 2011, have yet a different calculation of benefits. If the participant is retiring at their normal retirement date, the calculation of the annual pension benefit is:[52]

2.5 percent of the participant's highest average remuneration *times* the participant's number of years of service

plus

.25 percent of the participant's highest average remuneration *times* the participant's number of years of service up to 20 years.

The same minimum and maximum benefit regulations apply to these participants as participants hired on or after January 1, 2015.

PRACTICE TIP

A participant hired before September 30, 2011, will have a pension benefit calculated as follows (so long as they meet the other requirements for a pension benefit):

2.5 percent of the participant's highest average remuneration times ***the participant's number of years of service***

plus

.25 percent of the participant's highest average remuneration times ***the participant's number of years of service up to 20 years***

52. *Id.* Appendix VI, Section 4.1.

A participant with less than three years at the time of their termination of employment with the IDB will be paid their interest in the plan as a lump sum.[53] The lump sum is calculated as:[54]

10 percent of the participant's highest average remuneration *times* the number of qualified years of service

plus

4 percent of the participant's highest average remuneration *times* the number of years of qualified service.

A participant with at least three years of qualifying service before their normal retirement date may defer receipt of the pension benefit until as late as their normal retirement date.[55] If deferring to the normal retirement date, then the participant's benefit will not be reduced.[56] If the participant elects a start date prior to their normal retirement, the pension benefit will be reduced pursuant to the early retirement formulas that follow.[57]

A participant with at least three years of eligible service may also opt to receive their benefits as a withdrawal benefit.[58] If a participant elects for the withdrawal benefit and has up to and including eight years of service, the withdrawal benefit will be calculated as follows:

10 percent of their highest average remuneration *times* the number of years of eligible service

plus

12 percent of their highest average remuneration

plus

30 percent of their highest average remuneration for each year of service in excess of three years, up to eight years[59]

53. *Id.* Appendix VI, Section 4.10.
54. *Id.*
55. *Id.* Appendix VI, Section 4.4.
56. *Id.*
57. *Id.*
58. *Id.* Appendix VI, Section 4.10.
59. *Id.*

A participant with more than eight years of qualifying service will have their withdrawal benefit calculated as follows:

10 percent of their highest average remuneration *times* their number of years of qualifying service

plus

162 percent of their highest average remuneration at the end of their eighth year of qualifying service[60]

The participant that has more than eight years of eligible service can also defer to receive their interest in the plan as a pension benefit at their normal retirement date.

A special category of benefit calculation exists for participants hired between January 1, 1981, and December 31, 1996 (dates inclusive), pursuant to Resolution DC-161/96.[61] In the event these participants, upon termination of their employment with the IDB, elect to receive their benefits as a withdrawal benefit rather than a pension benefit, their withdrawal benefit is the higher of the withdrawal benefit calculation as of the date they terminate employment, or, the calculation that follows:[62]

> For participants with at least 36 months of eligible service and up to (and including) 72 months of service, the calculation is the participant's accumulated contributions, increased by 5 percent for each month of service over 36, up to 36 months of 180 percent of the accumulated contributions.
>
> For participants with at least 73 months of eligible service and up to (and including) 96 months of service, the calculation is the participant's accumulated contributions up to the last day of service *plus* 180 percent of the accumulated contributions.
>
> For participants with 97 months or more of eligible service, the calculation is the participant's accumulated

60. *Id.*
61. *Id.* Appendix V. Resolution DE-161/96.
62. *Id.* Appendix V.

contributions at the end of the participant's service *plus* 180 percent of the participant's accumulated contributions as of the end of the first 96 months of service.

Participants beginning service before January 1, 1981, have additional options for calculating their withdrawal benefit. These participants will receive the highest of the following calculations:[63]

1. The calculation as of the current iteration of the plan;
2. The calculation for participants hired between January 1, 1981, and December 31, 1996, with at least 36 but not more than 72 months of service; or
3. Their accumulated contributions *plus* 1 percent of the accumulated contributions *times* the number of months of eligible service, up to 180 months.

2.1.3.3.1 Early Retirement for Employees Hired on or Before September 30, 2011

The early retirement requirements are also different for participants hired on or before September 30, 2011. These participants are eligible for early retirement if they attain 50 years of age and have completed at least 15 years of qualifying service, or have attained 55 years of age and completed at least three years of qualifying service.[64] The retired participant will receive a percentage of the pension benefit they would be eligible for if they waited until their normal retirement date.[65] The percentage reduction is as follows:

Age at Benefit Commencement[66]	Percent of Pension Received
62	100%
61	97%
60	94%

63. *Id.*
64. *Id.* Appendix VI, Section 4.2(a).
65. *Id.*
66. Years are counted as full years only and are not prorated. *Id.*

Age at Benefit Commencement[66]	Percent of Pension Received
59	91%
58	87%
57	83%
56	79%
55	75%
54	70%
53	65%
52	60%
51	55%
50	50%

Alternatively, if the participant's age at the time of termination of employment and qualifying time of service, both calculated in months, equals 1,020 months, then the participant's benefit shall not be reduced.[67] If the participant's age and eligible service calculated in months is less than 1,020, then the participant will receive a reduced benefit according to the following table:[68]

Age Plus Service (in Months)	Percent of Pension Received
1,020	100%
996	97%
972	94%
948	91%
924	87%
900	83%

67. *Id.* Appendix VI. Section 4.2.
68. *Id.* Appendix VI, Section 4.2(b).

Age Plus Service (in Months)	Percent of Pension Received
876	79%
852	75%

Such early retirement pension shall begin to be paid on the first of the month next following the date the participant terminates their employment with the IDB.[69] In addition, if the participant's age in months plus months of service falls between categories listed in the preceding chart, the benefit will be prorated.[70] In other words, the benefit is calculated per employment period and then added together in terms of currency. This is different than the period of employment being cumulated and then the benefit calculated as if it were one large service period.

2.1.4 Restoration of Employment with the IDB

A participant may terminate employment with the IDB and later become re-employed with the IDB. If the participant elected for a deferred pension benefit at the termination of their first employment period with the IDB, then their pension benefit upon termination of their final employment period with the IDB will be calculated as the pension benefit for the first period of service *plus* the pension benefit for the second period of service, and so on for any additional periods of service.[71]

However, if the participant withdrew their benefit at the end of their first period of employment, then the participant's pension benefit will only be calculated based on the second and any future periods of employment.[72] If the participant desires to have their full amount of employment used for calculating their pension benefit, then they must make a full repayment of the withdrawal benefit they received, plus interest.[73]

---

69. *Id.* Appendix VI, Section 4.2(c).
70. *Id.*
71. *Id.* Section 5.1.
72. *Id.*
73. *Id.*

PRACTICE TIP

Participants who have received a withdrawal benefit upon termination of their employment with the IDB may repay the amount received with interest if they are subsequently re-employed with the IDB. If this happened in your case, then it is important to analyze whether the initial period of employment occurred during the marriage, and whether marital funds were used to repay the funds received to determine whether the retirement benefit at the IDB is marital.

2.1.5 Disability Pension

A participant may retire on disability while in participating service if the participant became totally incapacitated mentally or physically for the performance of the duties that the IDB may reasonably request of them to perform.[74] The incapacity must be likely permanent and therefore the participant should be retired by recommendation of physicians designated by the executive secretary.[75]

The disability pension shall be effective upon retirement, which shall begin no less than 30 days but no more than 120 days after an application being made by the participant to the executive secretary.[76] The amount of the disability pension is calculated as if the participant's normal retirement date falls on the date of the participant's disability retirement date, using the participant's actual years of eligible service and highest average remuneration.[77] Meaning that the participant will not receive an early retirement reduction should the disability require retirement prior to their normal retirement date. However, the disability pension shall not be less than 50 percent of the participant's highest average remuneration or the normal pension the

74. *Id.* Section 4.3.
75. *Id.*
76. *Id.*
77. *Id.* Section 4.3(b).

participant would have received upon their normal retirement date, with their actual highest average remuneration.[78]

A participant retired on disability may be required by the executive secretary to be medically examined no more than one time per year to confirm that the incapacity is ongoing.[79] If the disability pension is discontinued because it is determined that the incapacity is no longer in existence and it does not restart within five years, then the participant is considered to have withdrawn their interest in the plan for the eligible service accrued as of the date of the disability pension termination date.[80] In such event, the participant is entitled to either the pension benefits or withdrawal benefit, reduced for the amounts of disability pension received.[81]

2.1.6 Terminology

Accumulated Contributions.[82] The total of the participant's contributions plus the regular interest thereon.

The Bank.[83] The Inter-American Development Bank.

The Corporation.[84] The Inter-American Investment Corporation. Employees of the Corporation are participants in the IDB pension.

Date of Participation.[85] The date of participation for calculating a participant's lump-sum withdrawal benefit is the date on which the participant began their last period of service with the IDB. If the participant had previous service that was either restored or is eligible for deferred benefits it will be included in the calculation of benefits for amount of eligible service but will not impact the date of participation.

---

78. *Id.*
79. *Id.* Section 4.3(c).
80. *Id.* Section 4.3(e).
81. *Id.*
82. *Id.* Section 1.1(p).
83. *Id.* Section 1.1.
84. *Id.*
85. *Id.* Appendix V.

Eligible Service.[86] A participant accrues eligible service in the plan for any period in which the participant makes a contribution to the plan. Such periods shall include a leave of absence with pay, or any other leave approved by the IDB, so long as contributions are made.

Executive Secretary.[87] The executive secretary of the plan is appointed by the Bank. The executive secretary is responsible for overseeing the payment/distribution of all benefits under the plan, managing the investment of plan assets, and carrying out the day-to-day administration of the plan.[88]

Highest Average Remuneration (for Participants Hired on or Before December 31, 2014).[89] This is calculated by taking the highest average annual remuneration during the three consecutive years (not required to be calendar years) of service that result in the highest average. If the participant has less than three years of service with the IDB, then the total years of service shall be used for the calculation. In no event shall the average exceed the actual remuneration received during the same period.

Highest Average Remuneration (for Participants Hired on or After January 1, 2015).[90] This is calculated by (1) taking the five-year period (consecutive years, not required to be calendar years) of participating service during which the participant's unadjusted remuneration is the highest, or, if service is less than five years, the average of such service; (2) adjust the first four years for cost-of-living increases applied to pensions during such five-year period; and (3) take the average of the adjusted salaries. In no event shall such highest average remuneration exceed the participant's highest annual salary during the same five-year period.

Management Committee.[91] A committee appointed under the Pension Committee to administer the plan. The Management Committee

86. *Id.* Section 2.3.
87. *Id.* Section 1.1.
88. *Id.* Section 7.3.
89. *Id.* Appendix VII.
90. *Id.* Section 1.1(l).
91. *Id.* Section 1.1.

is comprised of the Vice President for Finance and Administration, the General Manager of the Human Resources Department, the Chief Financial Officer and General Manager of the Finance Department, the General manager of the Budget and Administrative Services Department, the Chief Risk Officer of the Office of Risk Management, the Chief Financial Officers of the Corporation, a member appointed by the Office of the Presidency of the Bank, and a member appointed by the Office of the Executive Vice President of the Bank.[92] The Management Committee is responsible for the administration of the plan and its application to participants, former participants, and others, and to determine whether a person has a right to benefits, and if so the amount thereof, and determine any question regarding the administration of the plan.[93]

Pension Committee.[94] A committee appointed to supervise the overall administration of the plan. The Pension Committee is comprised of the president of the Bank, the executive vice president of the Bank, the vice president for finance and administration, the general manager of the corporation, four other executive directors, as well as three staff members (and alternates) appointed by the president of the Bank, and two staff members elected biennially by the plan.[95] The Pension Committee determines the investment policy for the retirement fund that supports the plan, considering the risk profile of the Bank from time to time.[96]

Remuneration.[97] The regular *net* compensation paid to the participant by the IDB, excluding reimbursements for taxes, allowances, bonuses, overtime, special pay, separation payments, temporary salary increases, or lump-sum payments in lieu of annual leave. In the event a participant is on leave, the remuneration for such period is the annual remuneration received prior to taking leave. For employees hired after December 31, 1995, the maximum remuneration shall not

---

92. *Id.* Section 7.2(a).
93. *Id.* Section 7.2(b).
94. *Id.* Section 1.1.
95. *Id.* Section 7.1(a).
96. *Id.* Section 7.1(c).
97. *Id.* Section 1.1(k).

exceed the limits of the United States Internal Revenue Code of 1986, section 401(a)(17) as amended.

Remuneration of an Executive Director, Assistant Executive Director, Director of the Evaluation Office, Assistant to the Executive Director, or Part-Time Employee Who Has Completed Five Years of Service (Hired on or Before December 31, 2014).[98] The remuneration on which contributions were paid for the prior year, but not less than the participant's highest average remuneration. If service has been less than one year, than the remuneration shall be such period converted to an annual rate. For employees hired after December 31, 1995, the maximum remuneration shall not exceed the limits of the United States Internal Revenue Code of 1986, section 401(a)(17) as amended.

Retirement Date (Early). The date the retired participant elects to receive their benefit *prior to* their normal retirement date, so long as all requirements for early retirement are satisfied.

Retirement Date (Normal).[99] For participants hired on or after October 1, 2011, their normal retirement date is the first day of the calendar month next following the retired participant's 65th birthday, or the retired participant's 65th birthday, if the birthday is the first of the month. For participants hired on or before September 30, 2011, their normal retirement date is the first day of the calendar month next following the retired participant's 62nd birthday, or the retired participant's 62nd birthday if the birthday is the first of the month.[100]

Surviving Spouse.[101] A spouse who was married to the participant at the time of the participant's death and outlives the participant for at least ten days.

---

98. *Id.*
99. *Id.* Section 1.1(i).
100. *Id.* Appendix VI, Section 1.1(i).
101. *Id.* Section 4.5.

2.1.7 Form of Payment of Pension Benefits—Lump Sum / Commutation of Benefits

A retired participant[102] has the option to commute up to 50 percent of their pension benefit to a lump-sum payment.[103] Such lump-sum payment will be the actuarial equivalent of the commuted percent of the pension as of the date pension benefits commence, based on the actuarial tables adopted by the Pension Committee.[104] Payment of the commuted benefit will be made within 30 days of the commencement of pension benefits.[105] The commuted benefit shall not be reduced for any survivor benefit elected, however it shall reduce the amount of any survivor benefit available.[106]

PRACTICE TIP

A plan participant can commute up to 50 percent of their pension to a lump-sum payment. The spouse, court, or agreement cannot prohibit nor require the participant's ability to take a lump sum.

If the participant wants a commutation, the election therefor must be made at any time prior to the commencement of benefits. The election can be revoked or amended at any time prior to the commencement of pension benefits.[107] Any such election, amendment, or revocation must be made by written notice to the executive secretary.[108]

102. The retired participant must be eligible for a pension on early or normal retirement. A retired participant on a disability pension does not have this option. *Id.* Section 4.9.

103. *Id.*

104. *Id.*

105. *Id.*

106. *Id.* Section 4.9, Section 4.6(a).

107. *Id.* Section 4.9.

108. *Id.*

Distribution of pension benefits must begin no later than April 1 following the participant attaining age 70½.[109] Any benefits not commuted are paid in equal monthly installments.[110] However, the plan has the option to make payment of any benefit that is less than $120 per year in semiannual installments.[111] Payments are made at the end of the month, including in the month of the participant's death.[112]

2.1.8 Reimbursement for Taxes Paid

Each person receiving a pension benefit, either as a retired participant, surviving spouse, or child's benefit, shall also receive from the IDB an amount to cover national taxes levied on the payment amount from the pension.[113] The funds paid to cover taxes shall not be considered a pension payment or benefit for purpose of determining the minimum or maximum pension payments, nor taxable income pursuant to the U.S. Internal Revenue Code.[114]

A former spouse cannot waive this payment of funds to cover national taxes owed on the amount of the pension paid to the former spouse. In addition, the participant will continue to receive their own payment to cover national taxes owed on the pension paid to the participant. Neither party is harmed by such requirement.

PRACTICE TIP

While tax reimbursement is not a pension payment according to the plan, or the IRS, such funds can be considered income for purposes of calculating child support or alimony. Consult your local rules for guidance.

---

109. *Id.* Section 4.7(b).
110. *Id.* Section 4.7(a).
111. *Id.* Section 4.7.
112. *Id.*
113. *Id.* Section 13.8.
114. *Id.*

Jurisdictions differ in how they treat such payments with respect to income for child support or alimony purposes. For example, some jurisdictions allow only "actual income" received to be included for income purposes for alimony and/or child support. A tax payment may be considered income in those jurisdictions. What about jurisdictions that have a formula to "gross up" nontaxable income so that the income used for both parties is the pretax figure? In such a jurisdiction would this payment to cover national taxes be added and the figure grossed up even further? This is a very important consideration for parties where multiple jurisdictions are at issue.[115]

2.2 Pre-Retirement Survivor Benefit

If a participant dies while in the active employment of the IDB and has a surviving spouse, the IDB shall pay to the surviving spouse the survivor's pension.[116] The amount of such benefit will be one-half the amount of a disability pension the participant would have been eligible for as of the date of the participant's death.[117] However, the benefit shall not be less than the smaller of 25 percent of the participant's highest average remuneration or the total disability pension the participant would have received had they retired on a disability pension as of the date of death.[118]

---

115. Lemley v. Lemley, 102 Md. App. 266 (1994), *aff'd*, Ruiz v. Kinoshita, 239 Md. App. 392, 197 A.3d 47 (2018) (for Maryland citing that the courts do not have discretion to "gross up" or otherwise increase a party's income for taxes if the party receives nontaxable income for purposes of child support). D.C. Code § 16-916.01(d)(1)(X), which states that for purposes of child support "[t]axes paid on a party's income by an employer or, if the income is nontaxable, the amount of taxes that would be paid if the income were taxable." *In the Matter of Giacomini & Giacomini*, 150 NH 498 (NH 2004) (*stating* that the trial court did not abuse its discretion in excluding tax payments made by the employer to cover the employee's national and state taxes in a determination of a party's income). Portugal v. Portugal, 798 A.2d 246 (Pa. 2002) (*stating* that the court did not abuse discretion in excluding a one-time tax gross up payment by a party's employer in that party's income for child support purposes).

116. Staff Retirement Plan, *supra* note 5, Section 4.5.

117. *Id.*

118. *Id.*

PRACTICE TIP

The pre-retirement survivor benefit paid to a surviving spouse shall generally be one-half of the amount of the disability pension to which the employee would have been eligible.

The survivor's pension for a spouse may be waived if the participant can prove that it would be against the IDB's policies to make payment of the spouse pension. Examples the IDB provides for such circumstances are the parties are officially divorced by civil, ecclesiastical, or judicial authorities; the parties have reached a written agreement that establishes their permanent separation and dissolution of the marital relationship and financial interdependence typical of a married couple; or the participant is able to show some other kind of proof of a dissolution of the marriage and permanent separation.[119] If the parties agree to delay filing for divorce after reaching their agreement, both parties must be advised of the potential steps the other could take to frustrate this agreement.

If there is no surviving spouse to receive the benefit, then the designated beneficiary(ies) is/are eligible to share a lump-sum death benefit.[120] The lump-sum death benefit is calculated the same as the withdrawal benefit the participant would receive if they elected on the date of their death to receive a withdrawal benefit instead of a pension benefit.[121]

2.3 Post-Retirement Survivor Benefit

There are two types of post-retirement survivor pension available to the participant.

The first survivor benefit is the section 4.5 surviving spouse pension, which is called "survivors pension."[122] For ease in the section, we will call it the "4.5 survivor pension." This benefit is automatically created for a current spouse. There is no cost to the participant for

119. *Id.* Annex 1-4(1).
120. *Id.* Section 4.5(f).
121. *See* Section 2.1.3.1.1 herein.
122. Staff Retirement Plan, *supra* note 5, Section 4.5.

this benefit. There is no election or reduction made to affirmatively secure the 4.5 survivor pension. It is automatic.

The second survivor benefit is the "Section 4.6 survivor benefit." It is optional and may be created by election. It is referred to in the handbook as "Reduced Pension with Pension to Survivor."[123] This benefit is paid on the basis of actuarial reduction to the employee's pension. There is no easy calculation for the parties to understand how much the pension is decreased to provide this benefit. In general, though, the younger the survivor, the larger the reduction.

There is a cap on the combined pensions pursuant to sections 4.5 and 4.6 that may be created such that the participant must receive more from the portion of the pension payable to them than the sum of all the 4.5 and 4.6 survivor pensions available.[124] There appears to be no limit on the number of pensions that can be paid to survivors so long as this rule is not violated. Further, there appears to be no cap on the amount of the survivor pensions payable under section 4.5 and 4.6 combined, so long as the reduction to the participant's pension does not exceed 50 percent of the participant's pension benefit.

If the participant desires to commute a part of the employee pension, then the amount of pension benefit remaining after the commutation is what is split to create the employee pension and any other survivor pensions.[125] Since the entire benefit calculation is reduced, both the benefit to the participant and the survivor benefit are reduced by the commutation.[126] Payments to survivors begin in the month of the participant's death.[127]

PRACTICE TIP

In divorce, the 4.5 survivor pension is not divided as that is only for a surviving spouse. The 4.6 survivor benefit can be negotiated. Calculation of the cost of the 4.6 survivor benefit is not a simple, straightforward calculation.

123. *Id.* Section 4.6.
124. *Id.* Section 4.6(d).
125. *Id.* Section 4.6.
126. *Id.*
127. *Id.* Section 4.7.

If the participant wants to create a 4.6 survivor pension, the election must be made at any time prior to commencing pension benefits.[128] Such election is revokable until the participant begins to receive pension benefits.[129] If the person designated as a 4.6 survivor dies before the payments to this survivor begin, then the election is void and payments to the participant are made as if no election for a survivor pension was made.[130]

Two limits on the amount of the reduction to the participant's benefit exist. First, the participant cannot receive less than one-half the amount that they would have received had no election been made.[131] This means that a former spouse cannot receive both 50 percent of the pension benefits and any survivor benefit. If the former spouse is going to receive any survivor benefit, then they must receive less than 50 percent of the pension benefit due to the reduction to provide for the survivor pension.

PRACTICE TIP

The participant must receive at least 50 percent of the pension after all reductions for spousal survivor benefits and payments to former spouses. Therefore, a former spouse cannot receive both 50 percent of the entire pension benefit **and** ***survivor benefits.***

Second, the amount that the designated survivor is to receive from the survivor pension *plus* the amount that any other survivor is to receive in survivor benefits, including the spousal pension, must be less than the amount of the reduced pension payable to the participant.[132] Stated differently, the participant must receive more from the portion of the pension payable to them than the sum of all the survivor pensions payable.

---

128. *Id.*
129. *Id.*
130. *Id.*
131. *Id.* Section 4.6(d).
132. *Id.*

Due to these limits existing, it is important to submit a draft order to the IDB. As part of their review, they will check to ensure neither of these limits are being breached. If they are, the IDB will advise counsel of such, and counsel will be required to revise the draft order so it no longer violates the rule.

PRACTICE TIP

The plan will accept draft orders for review and comment. Due to all the variables and limitations, it is important to submit all retirement orders for preapproval.

2.3.1 Death Benefits

2.3.1.1 Lump-Sum Death Benefits

If the participant dies after beginning to receive pension benefits and without a surviving spouse, the designated beneficiary(ies) is/are entitled to two death benefit payments.[133]

The first is a refund of the participant's contributions made to the pension plan during their employment, *less* the gross amount of pension benefits received.[134] Specifically, if a participant elected to receive a reduced pension benefit to provide a larger survivor benefit for a surviving spouse, for example, then the unreduced amount of the payments that the participant would have received were it not for the survivor election will be deducted from the contributions.[135] In addition, if the participant received any pension benefits as a commuted sum, that amount will also be deducted from the contributions.[136]

The second death benefit payable to beneficiaries is a lump sum.[137] The lump sum is calculated as a percentage of the unreduced

---

133. Staff Retirement Plan, *supra* note 5, Section 4.5(f).

134. *Id.*

135. *Id.* This situation could arise if the participant had elected the survivor benefit, and the designated survivor predeceased the participant, thereby resulting in no survivor available to receive the survivor pension.

136. *Id.*

137. *Id.*

annual pension benefit the participant was eligible to receive.[138] The percentage of the pension is calculated as follows:[139]

Age at Birthday Nearest to Date of Death (Years)	Percent of Pension for Beneficiary
65 or younger	200%
66	180%
67	160%
68	140%
69	120%
70	100%
71	80%
72	60%
73 or older	50%

2.3.1.2 Children's Benefits

Upon the death of a participant or retired participant, there shall be a benefit payable to each unmarried child of said participant on a monthly basis until the child reaches age 21.[140] The children eligible for such benefit are those in existence at the time the participant terminated participated service with the IDB.[141] If there is still a living parent, the annual amount payable per child is $1,800, including cost-of-living increases.[142] If there is no living parent, then the annual amount payable for one child is the larger of $1,800 plus cost-of-living increases increased by 50 percent of itself, or increased by 25 percent of the amount the participant would have been entitled to receive on their death from the pension.[143] If there are two or more eligible children and no living parent, the benefit is the larger of the $1,800,

138. *Id.*
139. *Id.*
140. *Id.* Section 4.5(d).
141. *Id.*
142. *Id.*
143. *Id.*

including cost-of-living increases, or 50 percent of the participant's benefit.[144]

When a child becomes ineligible to continue receiving benefits, the total amount of benefits is redistributed among the remaining eligible children.[145] The amount of children's benefits cannot exceed the amount of any spouse's pension, or three eligible children.[146]

These benefits are not affected by or divisible by partition orders, divorce of the parties, or similar events. They similarly cannot be affected by any separate agreement of the parties.

2.4 Transfers to Other Institutions

The IDB has entered into agreements with other, similar plans to allow for the transfer of credits into and out of the IDB Staff Retirement Plan.[147] Specifically, the IDB has such agreements with the European Bank for Reconstruction and Development, the International Monetary Fund, the United Nations Joint Staff Pension Fund (and its member organizations[148]), and the World Bank.[149] In addition, the IDB SRP allows for transfers from the International Plan to the local plan, and vice versa.[150]

For transfers with the United Nations Joint Staff Pension Fund, the systems are so similar that they have determined the qualifying service is transferred on a one-to-one basis.[151] There is, however, an

---

144. *Id.*

145. *Id.*

146. *Id.*

147. *Id.* Section 4.8.

148. *See* Section 4.2.1 regarding UN joint staff pension fund member organizations.

149. IDB 2021 Annual Report SRP, at 41.

150. *Id.* The local plan is a plan extremely similar to the IDB SRP, however, its participants are IDB employees working at a field or country office, rather than for the headquarters office. The IDB local plan document and information can be found on the IDB website: https://www.iadb.org/en/extranet/retirees/retirees-pensions-plan#:~:text=The%20Local%20Retirement%20Plan%20(LRP,and%20a%20benefit%20accrual%20factor (last visited May 1, 2025).

151. Agreement between the United Nations Joint Staff Pension Board and the inter-America Development Bank on the continuity and transfer of pension rights of participants in the United Nations Joint Staff Pension Fund and of participants in the Staff Retirement Plan of the Inter-American Development Bank,

adjustment to the remuneration amount recorded for the participant in the new plan pursuant to a formula within the agreement.[152] A participant must elect in writing to the new plan to have their pension interest transferred from the old plan within six months of the termination of their participation in the old plan but no later than 90 days after beginning participation in the new plan.[153]

In terms of divorce and determining the former spouse's share of such benefit, for the IDB and the UN Joint Staff Pension Fund, no adjustment to the former spouse's share would need to be determined because the service time is transferred on a one-to-one basis. However, transfers between the IDB SRP and any other organization may require a more in-depth look into the transferred service time, to see if the former spouse's share needs to be adjusted to account for the difference. This means a traditional coverture fraction may not be an accurate way to divide the marital interest.

2.5 Division in Divorce

2.5.1 How to Divide the Employee Pension

Dividing the employee's pension benefit must be done through an order, described in Section 2.5.5 herein. The language provided by the IDB is naturally inclusive of both the employee's monthly pension benefits and any commuted amount. If the parties wish that only one of the two benefits be divided or that the former spouse receive a different share of monthly benefits than any commuted amount, then they will have to specify that in the order.

2.5.2 How to Divide the 4.6 Survivor Benefit

The 4.6 survivor benefit must be elected through a form at any time prior to the pension becoming payable, subject to the limits described in Section 2.3 herein.

1993; Transfer Agreement, United Nations Joint Staff Pension Fund, New York & Geneva, April 2005.

152. Agreement between UNJSPF and IDB.

153. *Id.*

2.5.3 Treatment of Post-Divorce Salary Adjustments

The IDB calculates the division based off of the participant's benefit as of their date of retirement or termination of participation with the plan. As such, any post-divorce salary adjustments are naturally included in the division of the participant's pension. This calculation cannot be changed.

2.5.4 Cost-of-Living Adjustments

Cost-of-living increases are calculated each year, and put into effect in January of each year.[154] Any pension effective after January 1, 1970, is eligible for cost-of-living increases.[155] Pensions are eligible for cost-of-living increases when payments begin, or in the case of deferred payments, when the participant leaves employment.[156] Generally, if a participant who has a deferred pension benefit returns to the employment of the IDB, the previously applied cost-of-living increases will be cancelled.[157] A court order must specify whether the former spouse's share of the pension shall be adjusted for cost-of-living increases.[158]

2.5.5 Orders—Request to Partition Benefits

A Qualified Domestic Relations Order (QDRO) is not enforceable against the IDB due to their privileges and immunities described in the book's Introduction under Privileges and Immunities. However, the IDB will honor court orders dividing pension benefits that follow the plan rules. The IDB will accept an order titled just about anything other than "QDRO" but suggests "Partition of Retirement Benefits Order" or "Order for Spousal Support."[159]

---

154. Staff Retirement Plan, *supra* note 5, Section 15.
155. *Id.*
156. *Id.*
157. *Id.*
158. Model Partition Order. IDB Commentary
159. *Id.*

PRACTICE TIP

A court order to divide the IDB SRP must not be called a Qualified Domestic Relations Order.

A court order to divide the IDB SRP must address the following items:

1. ***Amount awarded to the former spouse***
2. ***Whether the former spouse receives a share of any cost-of-living adjustments***
3. ***Whether the former spouse shall receive an amount to cover national taxes***
4. ***Whether the former spouse shall receive a share of any disability benefit***
5. ***Whether either party's remarriage shall impact payments to the former spouse***

The plan requires the following items to be agreed upon and stated in the order: the amount awarded to the former spouse; whether the former spouse's share shall be adjusted for cost-of-living increases; whether the former spouse shall receive an amount to cover national taxes on their benefit; whether the former spouse shall receive a share of the participant's disability benefit, if applicable; and whether the remarriage of either party terminates the payment of the benefits.[160] Note that courts may require additional information and the specific case may warrant additional terms to be included in the order, so these are minimum term requirements per the IDB only. At the very least, be sure to address each of these terms in any agreement or judgment of divorce.

The plan requires that the order state the participant is directing the plan to make such payments to the alternate payee.[161] The IDB prohibits reference to survivor benefits in the order dividing the SRP benefit. As such, if the alternate payee should receive such survivor benefit, then the language securing the benefit should be included in

160. *Id.*
161. *Id.*

the parties' agreement or other court order to ensure there is a means to enforce the participant's submission of the beneficiary form if necessary. Finally, the plan requires that the order include a statement that the order is not transferring any property rights in the plan to the alternate payee.[162]

PRACTICE TIP

The IDB plan prohibits the designation of beneficiary or any survivor benefits to the alternate payee within the order.

As far as process, the IDB prefers that the parties submit a draft order via email, so that the IDB can ensure that once the final, court-executed document reaches them, the order will be acceptable to the plan. The IDB also requires that the submitted draft be a mark-up of their model order, as a Word document, rather than a PDF or other un-editable type of document. The IDB will review the order and email it back with comments embedded in the document if anything needs to be revised or clarified. The IDB Managing Committee will not interpret any part of the order, so if any part is remotely vague, they will ask for clarification.

The Administration Committee will not accept petitions to change official records related to the following after the participant begins to receive pension benefits: participant or spouse's date of birth, participant's marriage, or child's date of birth.[163] This is important because the reductions to provide a survivor benefit are calculated actuarily, so if the spouse's age is improperly reported, the spouse (or former spouse) may not receive the amount they are entitled to. Similarly, a child's benefit can only be paid until the child reaches a certain age. If the child's age is reported incorrectly, payments may terminate early.

The former spouse can elect to receive their benefits as a direct rollover to an eligible retirement plan, if the partition order is a proper

---

162. *Id.*
163. Staff Retirement Plan, *supra* note 5, Annex 1-3.

domestic relations order pursuant to section 414(p) of the U.S. Internal Revenue Code.[164] The former spouse should consult with their financial advisor, however, to consider if this is a wise decision for their particular circumstances. Since the partition order can provide the former spouse with sufficient funds to pay national taxes on amounts received direct from the plan, the former spouse would be absolved of paying taxes on the income if received directly from the IDB. If rolled over to an eligible retirement plan in the alternate payee's name they will not be eligible for the national tax payment, and thus they will be responsible for national taxes at the time they take a distribution from said eligible retirement plan.

PRACTICE TIP

Just because the former spouse can elect to receive their benefits as a direct rollover to an eligible retirement plan, doesn't mean they should. A rollover means that the alternate payee will give up additional payments from the plan to cover national taxes on distributions. The former spouse should consult with a financial advisor to determine the best course of action for their financial needs.

2.5.6 Additional Forms

If the parties agreed that the alternate payee would receive any benefits upon the death of the participant, they must ensure that the participant promptly fills out and submits those forms to the plan. Since these benefits cannot be secured by the court order, the alternate payee may want the ability to request from the participant confirmation that they are still the current beneficiary.

---

164. *Id.* Section 4.7(c). If the former spouse decides to receive their post-retirement survivor benefit as a rollover, the actuarial equivalent of the benefit will be transferred to the account designated by the former spouse. This lump-sum payment is pretax, and thus if rolled into a traditional IRA, the former spouse will be taxed on the income when they remove the funds from the IRA, pursuant to the U.S. Tax Code.

The participant is also supposed to submit a direction to the plan directing them to make payment of the agreed upon amount to the alternate payee.[165] Although it is a reiteration of the information in the court order, the direction is still required. A direction is also irrevocable, unless a subsequent court order alters the terms and sufficient proof thereof is submitted to the plan.[166] Therefore, if representing the alternate payee, it will be important to include the award of any death benefits or beneficiary status in the direction, since it is irrevocable.

If the participant does not submit the direction, the alternate payee will have to submit a request to the plan. The request needs to include the same information as the direction. The participant will have 30 days to contest the request before the IDB accepts the request.

2.5.7 Contact Information

The final court order and any mailed correspondence should be directed to: Staff Retirement Plan of the Inter-American Development Bank, 1300 New York Avenue, NW, Mail Stop E0507, Washington, DC 20577. However, they can also be reached via email at VPF/SRP@iadb.org or 202-623-3560 for questions or the submission of draft orders. This contact information is for the office of the Executive Secretariat of the Retirement Plans. Many helpful people work in this office, and they will loop in other departments as necessary to address questions.

2.6 Remarriage of Employee

With respect to the regular pension benefits to be paid from the plan to the participant during their lifetime, the parties must decide whether the participant's remarriage will have an impact. The plan's order requires that such situation be considered and parties' agreement stated in the order, but it does not have a default stance.[167] Further, as the plan will not interpret the order, if it is not addressed in the order, the order will be rejected by the plan.

---

165. Staff Retirement Plan, *supra* note 5, Section 11.2.
166. IDB Model Order and Instructions.
167. *Id.*

As described in Section 2.2, Pre-Retirement Survivor Benefit, herein, a surviving spouse will receive a spousal benefit. The plan is clear that such surviving spouse takes precedence over any other beneficiary, and that there is only one surviving spouse.[168] If this is the participant's second marriage, then the parties will have to check what benefits were provided to the first spouse, and make sure that the current agreement will not be rejected by the IDB for leaving the participant with too small of a pension benefit.

It will be important to counsel your client about this information, regardless of which party you represent. If representing the non-employee in particular, the client should be advised in writing that even if they negotiate for being named a beneficiary to the participant's interest in the plan, such benefit can be lost if the participant remarries. Alternative methods of securing a death benefit for the former spouse should be considered if support after the participant's death is an important issue for the former spouse. Depending on the participant's health and age, a private life insurance policy may be a good option. Alternatively, beneficiary designations for other financial accounts come with no cost. Consulting with a financial planner may be beneficial to determine if post-death benefits are necessary.

If the participant remarries after beginning to receive benefits from the pension, the participant has the option to provide a spouse pension to the new partner.[169] Such election must be made in writing within 12 months of the date of marriage. The election becomes effective 24 months after being received by the plan.[170] Once the election becomes effective, the participant's pension payments are reduced.[171]

The reductions are subject to the same limits described in the Post-Retirement Survivor Benefit section herein.[172] However, if there is a violation of one of the limits, then the participant may make a payment to the plan so that the election of the spouse pension is not

168. Staff Retirement Plan, *supra* note 5, Section 4.5(f) "Upon the death of an active participant or of a retired participant who *is not survived by a spouse,* there shall be paid to the person or persons designated by him an amount determined[.]" (emphasis added).

169. *Id.* Section 4.6(d).

170. *Id.*

171. *Id.*

172. *Id. See also* Section 2.3 herein.

denied for violating the limit.[173] The payment must be made at least 60 days prior to the effective date of the election.[174] If the participant or the spouse so designated dies prior to the effective date of the election, then the election is void and any such payments made by the participant are returned to the participant or their estate.[175]

2.7 Remarriage of Alternate Payee

If the alternate payee gets remarried, the parties must decide how that marriage will impact the payment of benefits to the alternate payee. The plan simply requires that the parties state in the order what the impact of such an event is.[176] If the order is silent, it will be rejected. Generally, the purpose of the payments may help determine the result. If for alimony, are there local laws requiring that alimony payments terminate upon the recipient's remarriage? If for property division, is there any local guidance? This is as much an issue of state law as it is individual for each case.

PRACTICE TIP

You may add a provision to the order that states that payments to the alternate payee end in the event of their remarriage.

2.8 Special Considerations for Prenuptial Agreements

Current spouses take priority over former spouses in the eyes of the IDB as they relate to benefits from the plan. This view results in a current spouse having the ability to take benefits previously designated for the former spouse, so long as the participant remains married to this current spouse. Specifically, assume that upon divorcing his first wife, participant agreed to maintain this first wife as beneficiary of the

173. Staff Retirement Plan, *supra* note 5, Section 4.6(d).
174. *Id.*
175. *Id.*
176. IDB Model Order and Instructions.

plan, but not to divide the pension into two benefits (the benefit during the participant's lifetime and the survivor pension, as described in Section 2.3 herein). Then the first wife would only be eligible for lump-sum death benefits. However, there are no lump-sum death benefits to be paid if a spouse pension is paid. Therefore, if the participant gets remarried and the second wife does not waive interest in the spouse pension, the first wife will not receive her benefits upon the participant's death.[177]

In order for the IDB *not* to pay the spouse pension in the case of the prenuptial agreement, the agreement must establish "the permanent financial independence of the [participant] from the spouse and a waiver of the spouse's interest in any future pension benefits of the [participant]."[178] The participant must share the prenuptial agreement with the IDB once executed so the IDB knows not to make payment of the spouse pension if such agreement exists.

To waive interest entirely:

> *Sharon is an employee of the Inter-American Development Bank and has an interest in the IDB Staff Retirement Plan (SRP). In consideration of other benefits provided for Jim herein, as well as Jim being self-supporting from his own income and assets, Jim hereby waives any and all interest he may have in Sharon's IDB SRP now, or in the future, including any and all survivor benefits that he may otherwise become entitled to due to his marriage to Sharon.*

To waive interest in the survivor pension:

> *Chris is an employee of the Inter-American Development Bank and has an interest in the IDB Staff Retirement Plan (SRP). In consideration of other benefits provided for Carol herein, as well as Carol's ability to be self-supporting, Carol hereby waives any and all interest she may have in survivor benefits provided from Chris's IDB SRP.*

Although the language herein is geared for the IDB specifically, that is merely because the IDB provides guidance for this situation.

---

177. Staff Retirement Plan, *supra* note 5, Annex 1-4(1).
178. *Id.*

Since the other plans described herein similarly give preference to a current spouse over a former spouse as it relates to benefits (particularly death benefits) being paid from the plan, this is a good place to start with respect to any premarital agreement involving these plans.

2.9 Other Benefits

2.9.1 Health Benefits

The IDB provides a healthcare plan for employees located in the United States and Puerto Rico. This is called the International Plan. Effective January 1, 2023, Cigna Healthcare is the administrator for the medical, dental, and vision plan for the International Plan.[179] This is not health insurance coverage; rather it is a group medical benefits program, which is funded by participant and IDB contributions. The fund then covers a portion of the medical expense per the plan document.[180] Cigna Global is the administrator of the plan for participants living outside of the United States or Puerto Rico.[181]

The International Plan includes a medical, dental, vision, and prescription drug plan.[182] Premiums are determined by the IDB and payable by the participant.[183] The IDB requires that once eligible for Medicare, participants/retirees enroll in Medicare to maintain their IDB healthcare benefits.[184]

The International Plan states that a dependent child of divorced or separated parents will have as their primary insurance plan the plan of the parent ordered by the court to provide such coverage, and other plans will be secondary.[185] Further, a custodial parent's plan will be primary over a stepparent's plan.[186] Finally, a custodial parent's plan

---

179. https://www.iadb.org/en/extranet/medical-program/national-plan-medical-benefits (Feb. 8, 2023).

180. https://www.iadb.org/en/extranet/medical-program/national-plan-medical-benefits (Feb. 8, 2023).

181. *Id.*

182. Medical Benefits Program Handbook, Active and Retired Staff (Jan. 1, 2023).

183. *Id.* Section 1.3.

184. *Id.* 2.7.

185. *Id.* 7.4.5.

186. *Id.*

will be primary over the plan of a noncustodial parent's plan.[187] These are just the IDB plan's default rules for determining which insurance plan of a dependent child will be primary, and may be adjusted if other plans covering the child have other rules.

Participation in the IDB healthcare program is optional for children of the employee who do not qualify as dependent children for other IDB policies.[188] In addition, these children may remain on the employee's IDB plan whether or not they live with the employee, and until their 26th birthday.[189]

If an employee dies while in active service and was covered by the health program at the time of death and the surviving spouse begins to receive the survivor's pension from the IDB SRP, then the surviving spouse will be eligible to continue coverage under the IDB health plan.[190] The premium will be calculated as if the employee had been employed by the IDB for five years, or their actual term of service, whichever is greater.[191]

A retired employee has the option of maintaining coverage under the IDB health program based on their entitlement to a pension benefit.[192] If the retiree decides to discontinue enrollment in the IDB plan, such decision is irrevocable and prevents any dependent children or spouse to continue on the program as well.[193]

2.9.2 Continuation of Health Insurance for a Former Spouse After the Marriage

Coverage for the former spouse and formerly dependent child will continue at no cost to the employee for 30 days after the child is no longer a dependent or the date of divorce or effective date of the Declaration of Termination of Domestic Partnership.[194] There is no fur-

187. *Id.*
188. *Id.* 3.2.1.2.
189. *Id.*
190. *Id.* 10.1.
191. *Id.* 10.1.2.
192. *Id.* PE-375 Annex 1, Vesting Criteria for the Retiree Medical Insurance Program.
193. *Id.*
194. *Id.* Section 6.2.1.

ther continuation of health benefits for the former spouse after the divorce.

A surviving spouse who is receiving a pension from the IDB SRP and who continues their enrollment in the IDB health program may continue to maintain their dependent children (who are also the children of the deceased employee) as covered participants for so long as they are eligible.[195] The surviving spouse may remarry or enter into a new domestic partnership and maintain their enrollment in the IDB health program, however, their new spouse/domestic partner and any children with the new spouse/domestic partner are not eligible for coverage under the IDB health program.[196]

PRACTICE TIP

The former spouse will only receive 30 days of additional health insurance coverage after the divorce. There is no option to receive additional health insurance coverage as a former spouse through the IDB.

2.9.3 Life Insurance

The IDB provides life insurance and accident and disability insurance coverage. Contact the IDB HR Department for additional information if desired for your case.

2.9.4 Benefits for Families Stationed Overseas

For families stationed overseas, there are certain benefits that make the relocation more attractive. For expatriate staff assigned to headquarters, there is an education benefit in which the employee's children within the age range of 5 to 25 can receive up to 75 percent of their basic education costs covered and up to 50 percent of their college tuition covered.[197] The payment occurs at the end of each

195. *Id.* Section 5.2.3.

196. *Id.*

197. IDB Global Federal Credit Union, https://www.idbglobalfcu.org/loans/student-loans.htm#basic (last visited May 12, 2025).

academic year and can include reimbursement for room and board and other related costs.[198]

2.9.5 Travel Expenses

For staff stationed internationally, the IDB provides several travel benefits. One benefit includes an appointment and relocation travel allowance that covers the cost of relocation for the staff member and their eligible dependents.[199] Once the staff member is stationed, the IDB provides a home country travel allowance that allows the employee and their eligible dependents to visit their country of origin.[200] This benefit is paid for every two years of service the IDB employee performs.[201] Finally, there is a repatriation travel benefit that finances the employee's relocation back to their point of origin.[202] This includes financial assistance for the employee's travel, as well as their eligible dependents.[203]

198. *Id.*
199. *Id.*
200. *Id.*
201. *Id.*
202. *Id.*
203. *Id.*

Chapter 3

World Bank

3.1 World Bank

The World Bank Group (WBG) is an international organization consisting of five institutions: the International Bank for Reconstruction and Development (IBRD), the International Development Association (IDA), the International Finance Corporation (IFC), the Multilateral Investment Guarantee Agency (MIGA), and the International Centre for Settlement of Investment Disputes (ICSID).[1] Each of these institutions has its own mission, membership, governing board, and operating agreement.[2] However, they work together to achieve goals and to have a greater impact.[3]

Membership within the World Bank is conditional upon membership in the IMF. The president of the World Bank is historically an American citizen, while the managing director of the IMF is historically a European citizen.[4] The United States also has the largest voting power in the World Bank, holding 15.4 percent of the votes, which is nearly twice the amount of the second largest voting power holder,

1. World Bank Group, *Who We Are*, https://www.worldbank.org/en/who-we-are (last visited May, 1, 2025).

2. *Id.*

3. *Id.*

4. *Selecting the World Bank President*, Congressional Research Service (May 10, 2023). Noting that this informal agreement regarding the nationality of these two positions is becoming a point of contention recently as more countries are playing a larger role in the global economy and it may unnecessarily favor nationality over merit-based qualifications.

Japan.[5] At the end of fiscal year 2022, the World Bank employed 12,778 full-time employees, 54 percent of which were employed at the Washington, D.C., headquarters location.[6] The World Bank's website is www.worldbank.org, and their logo is:

THE WORLD BANK

3.2 Overview of World Bank Pension

3.2.1 How It Works/Funding

The World Bank pension plan is in fact three pension funds. The main fund is the Staff Retirement Plan and Trust (SRP).[7] It was created in 1948 and officially approved by the IBRD as a trust in 2001. The other two pension funds are the Retired Staff Benefits Plan and Trust (RSBP) and the Post-Employment Benefits Plan (PEBP).[8]

The SRP is a funded contributory defined benefit plan.[9] The funds are held in trust, and the trustee is the IBRD who manages the investments and pays the expenses of the trust.[10]

The SRP consists of two components, the defined benefit (DB) component and the cash balance (CB) component.[11]

The DB component is funded entirely by the World Bank Group.[12] The DB component provides a defined benefit at the participant's normal retirement age. The benefit is calculated as 1 percent *times* years of participation *times* the participant's highest consecutive

5. International Bank for Reconstruction and Development Subscriptions and Voting Power of Member Countries (May 2, 2023). Voting power is determined by base votes and the share of the capital stock held by the member country. *Id.*

6. World Bank Annual Report, 2022, at 83.

7. WB SRP Brief.

8. *Id.* These plans are not discussed in this book.

9. *Id.*

10. *Id.*

11. HQ Staff Brochure (June 2018), https://thedocs.worldbank.org/en/doc/577621554749161719-0220012019/original/MyBenefitsHeadquartersStaffBrochure.pdf.

12. *Id.*

three years of average net salary and is paid in the currency of the participant's salary.[13]

The CB component is funded both by the WBG and the participant.[14] The WBG contributes an amount equal to 10 percent of the Participant's net salary paid to the participant that month.[15] The Participant contributes a mandatory 5 percent of their net salary each month and has the option to contribute up to 6 percent more.[16] A participant by default is contributing this optional six percent unless they elect otherwise.[17]

In addition to the WBG and participant's contributions to the CB benefit, the rate of return for the investments is called deemed earnings, which is also credited to the participant's CB benefit.

The funds within the account are invested at the option of the participant, so the account balance will change with the investments.[18] If the participant does not make any investment elections, then the funds will be invested in the "Real 3%,"[19] which is the WBG's most conservative fund option.[20] The participant retains the right to reinvest the funds.

These three contribution sources (WBG contributions, participant contributions, and investment earnings) make up what the WBG calls the CB accumulated balance.[21]

3.2.2 Who Is Eligible to Participate

Employees hired for regular, open-ended,[22] or term[23] appointments, as well as the President of the World Bank, are required to participate

---

13. *Id.*
14. *Id.*
15. SRP, Article 3.5(c).
16. *Id.* Article 3.5(d)(2).
17. *Id.*
18. *Id.*
19. *Id.*
20. *Communication with Kennedy Odenti at WGB sometime in 2022.*
21. *See* Terminology, Section 3.1.4 herein.
22. Open-ended terms are without a specified length. These are not offered frequently and are typically on a case-by-case basis. WBG Staff Directive 4.01 – Appointment.
23. *Id.* Term appointments are for a fixed length of time. The minimum term is one year and the maximum term is five years. Term appointments are renewable.

in the Pension/Staff Retirement Plan (SRP).[24] An employee hired as an executive director, an alternate executive director, or an advisor or senior advisor to an executive director has the choice to opt-out of participation in the SRP.[25] All such employees are a participant in the Net Plan if they were never a participant before April 15, 1998, or they were a participant prior to April 15, 1998, but they received a withdraw benefit for such service.[26] Alternatively, an employee will be a member of the Gross Plan if they were an employee at any time prior to April 15, 1998, and did not receive a withdrawal benefit prior to any continuation or restored service thereafter.[27]

PRACTICE TIP

The Gross Plan is generally for employees participating before April 15, 1998. The Net Plan is generally for employees hired on or after April 15, 1998.

3.2.3 Eligibility for Retirement/ Vesting

3.2.3.1 Gross Plan

The Gross Plan is the WBG's older retirement system, and applies to participants prior to April 15, 1998, who did not receive a withdrawal benefit and later resume employment with the WBG.

3.2.3.1.1 Normal Retirement

The normal retirement age for a Gross Plan participant is 62. A participant may receive their normal retirement benefit if they terminate employment with the WBG (other than by death) on or after their

---

24. WB Domestic Relations Manual, Section 2.13.

25. SRP, Article 2.2(c). If these employees opt-out of participation, then such election must be made within the first six months of employment, and the election will be effective as of the first day of employment. *Id.*

26. *Id.* Article 2.1.

27. *Id.* Article 9.1.

62nd birthday.[28] A participant may begin to receive their normal pension sooner than age 62 if after April 15, 1998, the Gross Plan participant meets the following conditions:[29]

1. Is at least 50 years old *or* has completed at least three years of service;
2. On April 14, 1998, was in contributory service with the WBG or was in a period of approved leave without pay;
3. Has not received a severance payment or withdrawal benefit upon termination of employment; and
4. Elects to begin to receiving benefits prior to attaining age 62.

For a Gross Plan participant whose entire tenure with the WBG is on or after May 1, 1990, the normal retirement benefit is computed as follows, however such benefit may not be greater than 73 percent of the participant's highest average gross salary:[30]

2.2 percent of the highest average gross salary *times* the number of years of service up to 25 years

plus

1.8 percent of the highest average gross salary *times* the number of years of service in excess of 25 years

3.2.3.1.2 Early Retirement

A Gross Plan participant who has at least three years of service may begin to receive their pension as early as age 55.[31] Doing so, however, will reduce the pension calculation by the smaller of:[32]

---

28. WBG, Article 10.2(a).
29. WBG SRP, Article 10.4(a).
30. WBG, Article 10.2(b) & (c). Gross Plan participants employed before May 1, 1990, have a different calculation for their pension benefit, and may have other benefits than those described herein, and depending on the participant's actual date of employment may have a normal retirement date of 65 years old. WBG SRP, Article 27, Schedule B. These benefits are not discussed within this book, though materials are with the authors in the event it is helpful to any reader.
31. WBG SRP, Article 10.3.
32. *Id.* Article 10.3(a)(2).

1. 3/365 of 1 percent for each day between the date benefits commence and the participant's normal retirement age; or
2. 3/730 of 1 percent for the difference of 31,025 minus the sum of the participant's age in days as of the date benefits commence and the amount of the participant's service in days.

Alternatively, a Gross Plan participant may begin to receive their benefits at age 50, if their age in days plus their number of days of service equals at least 27,375 and they retire for reasons other than death or disability.[33] This is called the Rule of 75. A participant beginning their benefits under this rule will have their pension reduced by 5/365 of 1 percent for each day between the benefit commencement date and the participant's 55th birthday.[34]

3.2.3.1.3 Survivor and Death Benefit Options

3.2.3.1.3.1 Pre-Retirement Death Benefits

If the participant is still employed with the WBG and has a surviving spouse or domestic partner at the time of death, then that surviving spouse or domestic partner shall receive an annuity for life unless the participant opted for such person to receive a lump sum.[35] Such election does not require spousal consent. The amount of the surviving spouse or domestic partner's annuity is calculated as follows:[36]

1. If the participant were to receive a disability pension as of the date of death and the value of that disability pension would have been more than 60 percent of their highest average gross salary, then their surviving spouse or domestic partner's pension shall be 50 percent of such disability pension.
2. If the participant were to receive a disability pension as of the date of death and the value of that disability pension would have been between 30 percent and up to but not including 60 percent of their highest average gross salary, then the surviving spouse or domestic partner's pension shall be 30 percent of the participant's highest average gross salary.

---

33. *Id.* Article 10.3(b).
34. *Id.* Article 10.3(b).
35. *Id.* Article 11.2(a).
36. *Id.*

3. If the participant were to receive a disability pension as of the date of death and the value of that disability pension would have been less than 30 percent of their highest average gross salary, then the surviving spouse or domestic partner's pension shall be the amount of the disability pension.

If the participant is no longer employed with the WBG but has not yet begun to receive their pension benefits at the time of their death and has a surviving spouse or domestic partner at the time of death, then the benefit payable to the surviving spouse or domestic partner is 50 percent of what would have been paid to the participant on the later of the participant's death or the participant's 55th birthday.[37]

If the participant is still employed by the WBG at the time of their death and does not have a surviving spouse or domestic partner, then the participant's designated beneficiary shall receive a lump-sum payment in the amount of:[38]

The participant's accumulated contributions to the plan

plus

Two times the amount of the participant's highest gross salary as of the earlier of age 62 or the date of death.

If the participant does not have a surviving spouse or domestic partner at the time of the participant's death prior to age 55 or the participant is receiving a reduced early retirement pension, then the lump-sum amount shall be equal to the amount of the withdrawal benefit the participant could have received had the withdrawal benefit been elected at the time of the participant's death or termination of service.[39]

If the participant does not have a surviving spouse or domestic partner at the time of the participant's death after age 55, then the lump-sum payment shall be calculated as follows:[40]

37. *Id.* Article 11.2(a)(ii).
38. *Id.* Article 11.2(b)(i).
39. *Id.* Article 11.2(b)(ii).
40. *Id.* Article 11.2(b)(iii).

The participant's accumulated contributions as of the date of death

plus

A percentage of the pension the participant would have received prior to the reduction for an optional survivor's pension or commutation of benefits.

The percentage of the pension payable is pursuant to the following chart:[41]

Age at Death	Percent of Pension
65 or younger	200%
66	180%
67	160%
68	140%
69	120%
70	100%
71	80%
72	60%
73 or older	50%

3.2.3.1.3.2 Post-Retirement Survivor and Death Benefits

If a participant who is already receiving their pension benefit dies with a surviving spouse or domestic partner *who was also married to the participant on their last day of participation in the plan*, that surviving spouse or domestic partner's pension shall be 50 percent of the participant's pension.[42]

If a participant who is already receiving their pension benefit dies without a surviving spouse or domestic partner then their beneficiary(ies) shall receive a lump sum totaling:[43]

41. *Id.* Article 11.2(b).
42. *Id.* Article 11.2(a)(ii).
43. *Id.* Article 11.2(b)(iii).

The participant's accumulated contributions as of the date of death

plus

A percentage of the pension the participant would have received prior to the reduction for an optional survivor's pension or commutation of benefits.

The percentage of the pension payable is pursuant to the following chart:[44]

Age at Death	Percent of Pension
65 or younger	200%
66	180%
67	160%
68	140%
69	120%
70	100%
71	80%
72	60%
73 or older	50%

The retiree may elect for an optional survivor's pension if they are married during retirement, divorced during retirement, or there is a birth/adoption during retirement.[45] The retiree's pension will be reduced to allow for the survivor pension, and the election must be made within 180 days of the event's occurrence.[46]

The retiree's pension will be reduced only once the election for the survivor's pension becomes effective.[47] An election to provide such survivor pension to a new spouse will become effective one year

44. *Id.* Article 11.2(b).
45. *Id.* Section 11.3(a).
46. *Id.*
47. *Id.* Section 11.3.

after the date of marriage.[48] An election to provide the survivor pension to the former spouse will become effective one year after the divorce is final, or 60 days after the election form is received by the plan administrator, whichever last occurs.[49]

PRACTICE TIP

The election for a former spouse survivor benefit becomes effective one year after the date of divorce, or 60 days after the election form is received by the plan administrator, whichever last occurs.

The WBG requires that at a minimum, after all reductions to a participant's pension benefit for division with (a) former spouse(s), and reductions for any survivor benefits, the participant receive 50 percent of their unreduced benefit. For example, a former spouse cannot receive both 50 percent of the pension benefit during the participant's lifetime and a survivor benefit. The former spouse's share during the participant's lifetime would have to decrease to allow for the survivor benefit, or the former spouse would not receive a survivor benefit.

The WBG will advise counsel and parties if a drafted order violates this prohibition upon review of a draft order. It is also important that if this is not the participant's first marriage, that counsel determine if, or how much of, the WBG pension was awarded to a previous spouse.

3.2.3.2 Net Plan

3.2.3.2.1 Normal Retirement

Participants who began participating in the Net plan on or before December 30, 2015, have a normal retirement age of 62 years.[50] Participants who began to participate in the Net Plan on or after December

48. *Id.*
49. *Id.*
50. HQ Staff Brochure, *supra* note 11.

31, 2015, have a normal retirement age of 65 years and have completed at least 3,650 days of service or have completed at least 1,825 days of service and whose age (in days) plus days of service equals at least 21,900.[51] Participants beginning participation on or after December 31, 2015, also includes participants who had received a withdrawal benefit (see Section 4.6) for participation completed prior to December 31, 2015. Participants beginning to receive their benefits upon reaching their normal retirement age are eligible for full, unreduced benefits.[52] The age 65 requirement is subject to change by the WBG prior to the participant's retirement date.[53]

The amount of the normal pension is calculated as 1 percent of the participant's highest average net salary *times* the number of days of service *divided by* 365.[54] However, the maximum pension benefit is 35 percent of the participant's highest average net salary.[55] This calculation is used to determine the participant's benefit from the defined benefit portion of the pension only.

3.2.3.2.2 Early Retirement

Participants terminating service with the WBG prior to their normal retirement date but having completed at least 3,650 days of service or having completed at least 1,825 days of service and whose age (in days) plus days of service equals at least 21,900 are eligible for a deferred pension benefit.[56] Alternatively, the participant may begin to receive their pension benefits as early as age 50, with a reduction.[57] The reduction is 3/365 of 1 percent for each day between the date the participant commences benefits and the participant's normal retirement date.[58]

---

51. *Id.*
52. *Id.*
53. SRP, Article 3.2(a).
54. *Id.* Article 3.2(b).
55. *Id.* Article 3.2(c).
56. *Id.* Article 3.3(a).
57. *Id.* Article 3.3(b) & (c).
58. *Id.* Article 3.3(c).

3.2.4 Terminology

Cash Balance (CB) Benefit.[59] A notional account creating the record of deemed employer contributions, participant contributions, and deemed earnings. It is not an actual account, nor does it provide any claim to particular assets in the SRP for the participant.

Deemed Employer Contributions.[60] Credits to the participant's cash balance benefit in the amount of 10 percent of the participant's net salary that month. A disabled participant will be credited with 21 percent of their monthly net salary.

Defined Benefit (DB) Component.[61] The component of the retirement benefit that provides a sum certain annual benefit to the participant, the amount of which is determined by formula.

Domestic Partner.[62] An unmarried individual whom the participant, while unmarried and in service in the plan has registered with the employer as the participant's domestic partner. A participant can have only one domestic partner at a time.

Highest Average Net Salary.[63] The participant's average annual net salary during 1,095 consecutive days of service that produce the highest such average. If there is a break in the participant's service, the period before and after the break shall be treated as consecutive for this purpose.

Participant Contributions.[64] Credits to the participant's cash balance benefit taken from the participant's net salary. These credits can take the form of mandatory, optional, or additional contributions as described herein.

Surviving Domestic Partner.[65] An individual who is the domestic partner of the participant at the time of the participant's death and who outlives the participant.

---

59. *Id.* Article 3.5(b).
60. *Id.* Article 3.5(c).
61. HQ Staff Brochure, *supra* note 11.
62. *Id.* Article 1.1(aa)
63. *Id.* Article 1.2(e).
64. SRP Article 3.5(d).
65. *Id.* Article 1.1 (bb)

Surviving Spouse.[66] An individual who is married to the participant or retired participant at the time of the participant or retired participant's death and who outlives the participant or retired participant.

Termination Grant.[67] A payment equal to 14 percent of the participant's final net salary times the number of years of termination grant service completed. Termination grant service is the amount of time a participant was employed with the WBG prior to April 15, 1998, in a local, regular or local, or fixed term appointment.

3.2.5 Lump Sum/Conversion of Benefits

The participant is eligible to receive the DB component as a monthly benefit if they have at least ten years of service, or they have at least five years of service and their age plus years of service is equal to or greater than 60.[68] If a participant does not meet these requirements to receive their DB component benefits as a monthly pension, then the benefits *will* be paid as a lump sum upon termination of employment.[69] The formula to determine the lump sum benefit of the DB Component is: 8 percent *times* years of participation *times* the participant's highest consecutive three years of average net salary.[70]

PRACTICE TIP

A participant is eligible to receive their DB component as a lump sum if they have at least ten years of eligible service, or they have at least five years of eligible service and their total years of service plus their age is greater than or equal to 60.

If the participant does meet these requirements to receive the DB component as a monthly pension but is not yet age 50, then the

66. Staff Retirement Plan and Trust of the International Bank for Reconstruction and Development. Incorporating amendments adopted on or before July 1, 2023. Article 1.1 (g).

67. WBG SRP Article 4.7.

68. HQ Staff Brochure, *supra* note 11.

69. *Id.*

70. *Id.*

participant *may* receive their benefits as a lump sum.[71] Spousal consent is required to receive the DB component benefit as a lump sum if the participant is eligible (or will be upon reaching retirement age) for a monthly pension benefit.[72]

PRACTICE TIP

If a participant is to receive their DB component as a lump sum, it is calculated as 8 percent times the participant's years of participation time the participant's highest consecutive three years of average net salary.

A participant *will* receive their CB component as a lump sum if they elect or are required to receive their DB component as a lump sum.[73] If this is the case, then no further benefits will be paid out to the participant's spouse or other beneficiary or dependent of the participant in the future.[74]

PRACTICE TIP

If the participant receives their DB component as a lump sum they will be required to receive the CB component as a lump sum. If they receive 100 percent of each benefit as a lump sum, there will not be any other benefits available from the plan, including survivor benefits.

A participant who is eligible to receive and in fact does receive their DB component as a monthly pension has the option to receive up to 100 percent of their CB component as an annuity.[75] Participants

71. *Id.*
72. *Id.*
73. *Id.*
74. *Id.*
75. *Id.*

opting to receive all or a part of their CB component as an annuity will receive it in the same form and currency as their DB component.[76]

To convert the CB component to an annuity, the WBG divides the amount of the CB component being converted by a "conversion factor."[77] The WBG defines this conversion factor as the "cost of buying $1 of an annual pension at a specific retirement age . . . [t]he younger [the annuitant is] the more expensive [the conversion] is, considering the longer life expectancy."[78] Specifically, the WBG uses the following chart to convert a CB component to an annuity, based on the participant's age as of the date they commence pension benefits:[79]

Age on Date of Benefit Commencement	Annuity Conversion Factor
50	20.952
51	20.647
52	20.337
53	20.020
54	19.695
55	19.368
56	19.036
57	18.693
58	18.342
59	17.981
60	17.613
61	17.233
62	16.846
63	16.455

76. *Id.*
77. *Id.*
78. *Id.*
79. WBG SRP, Schedule B, Table 5.

Age on Date of Benefit Commencement	Annuity Conversion Factor
64	16.058
65	15.656
66	15.252
67	14.842
68	14.427
69	14.006
70	13.580
71	13.149
72	12.718

The value of the participant's CB component is divided by the annuity conversion factor listed in the preceding table to determine the annual annuity amount.[80] If a participant is not exactly the age listed, their age is rounded such that any amount of months fewer than six shall be disregarded so the participant's age is rounded down, and any amount of months over six shall be included so the participant's age is rounded up.[81]

If a participant opts to have less than the full CB component converted to an annuity, the remaining balance will be paid as a lump sum.[82]

3.3 Death Benefit Options

3.3.1 Normal Form of Death Benefit

The WBG describes the normal form of death benefit to be a single life annuity for the plan participant and a death benefit.[83] The default form of the death benefit will be either a lump sum or a survivor

80. *Id.*
81. *Id.*
82. *Id.*
83. WBG SRP (2023), Article 4.2(a).

annuity, depending on the beneficiary's relationship with the participant, however, the form can be changed.[84] Specifically, the default form for a surviving spouse or surviving domestic partner is a survivor annuity, whereas the default form or any other beneficiary is a lump sum.[85]

3.3.2 Death with a Surviving Spouse or Surviving Domestic Partner (Not Former Spouse)

Although these definitions are listed in the terminology section, they are important, and therefore bear repeating here. A "surviving spouse" is someone who is married to the participant as of their last day of service in the Net Plan, remains married to that person through the commencement of the participant's pension benefits, and outlives the participant by at least 30 days.[86] A former spouse is not a "surviving spouse" (see Section 3.3.1 for information on a former spouse survivor pension). A surviving domestic partner is someone who is registered with the WBG as the participant's domestic partner as of the participant's last day of service in the Net Plan.[87]

PRACTICE TIP

A surviving spouse is someone who is married to the participant as of their last day of service in the Net Plan, remains married to that person through the commencement of the participant's pension benefits, and outlives the participant by at least 30 days.[88]

If a participant with a surviving spouse or surviving domestic partner dies while still in service with the WBG, the surviving spouse or domestic partner has the option of receiving their benefits as a survivor's annuity, or a lump sum, or a combination of the two.

84. *Id.* Article 4.2(b).
85. *Id.*
86. *Id.* Article 4.4(a)(v)(1).
87. *Id.* Article 4.4(a)(v)(2).
88. *Id.* Article 4.4(a)(v)(1).

The amount of the survivor's annuity is 30 percent of the participant's highest average net salary as of the participant's death.[89] However, it cannot be smaller than 50 percent of the participant's accrued pension benefit as of the date of the participant's death *plus* the value of the participant's cash balance benefit and termination grant when converted to an annuity.[90] Further, the amount of the survivor's pension cannot be larger than 2.45 percent of the participant's highest average net salary *times* the participant's number of days of service projected through age 65 *divided by* 365.[91]

PRACTICE TIP

There may be more than one surviving spouse in the event of polygamy.

The amount of the lump-sum option is:

two times the participant's final net salary

plus

8 percent of the participant's highest average net salary as of the date of death *times* the number of days of service *divided by* 365

plus

the value of the participant's cash balance account as of the first day of the month of the participant's death

plus

the value of the termination grant that would have been payable to the participant on the date of death.[92]

---

89. *Id.* Article 4.4(b)(i).

90. *Id.* Article 4.4(b)(i)(1). Specifically, the conversion rate is pursuant to SRP Article 26, Schedule B, Table 5, as of the date of the participant's death or age 65, whichever last occurs.

91. *Id.* Article 4.4(b)(i)(1)(2).

92. *Id.* Article 4.4(b)(ii).

If a participant dies with more than one surviving spouse, the Administration Committee has absolute discretion to award the death benefits to any of the surviving spouses entirely, or to divide it between them.[93]

If a participant dies while in deferred retirement with a surviving spouse or domestic partner, said surviving spouse or domestic partner shall have the option to elect either a survivor annuity or a lump-sum benefit.

In this case, the amount of the survivor's annuity is calculated pursuant to the WBG SRP Article 26, Schedule B, Table 2A or 2B as applicable, based on the age of the participant and the survivor, and the participant's date of hire *plus* the value of the participant's cash balance benefit and termination grant, converted to an annuity.[94] Alternatively, the amount of the lump sum is calculated as follows:

8 percent of the participant's highest average net salary as of the date of death (including any cost-of-living adjustments) *times* the participant's number of days of service divided by 365

plus

the participant's cash balance account as of the first of the month of the participant's death

plus

the participant's termination grant as of the date of death

In either of the scenarios in which the participant dies with a surviving spouse or domestic partner, the default payment form is a survivor annuity. The participant may reduce their share of the pension benefits to increase the amount of the survivor annuity.[95] If, however, the participant elects for their surviving spouse or domestic partner to receive a lump-sum payment instead, the participant cannot reduce their share of the pension benefit to increase the lump-sum payment to their survivor.

---

93. *Id.* Article 4.4(a)(vi).
94. *Id.* Article 4.4(d)(i). See Appendix 1 herein for full chart.
95. *Id.* Article 4.2(d).

A surviving spouse takes precedence over a designated beneficiary with respect to death benefits.[96] This precedence means that if the participant remarries before beginning to receive benefits from the Net Plan, the former spouse will not receive any death benefits from the WBG, even if the former spouse is the designated beneficiary. The only exception is if the participant agrees to purchase an increased survivor annuity.

PRACTICE TIP

If the participant remarries before beginning to receive benefits from the Net Plan that spouse will automatically be the beneficiary of the surviving spouse pension and any death benefits. The new spouse would have to waive such benefits in order for the former spouse to receive them, unless the participant elected to provide an optional former spouse survivor pension as described in Section 3.3.

A beneficiary designation as well as a decision to provide a survivor with a survivor annuity or lump-sum payment becomes irrevocable upon the date pension benefits commence.[97] As such, if the divorce involves a party already receiving their WBG pension, survivor benefits are not worth discussing as a part of the negotiation since they cannot be changed.

PRACTICE TIP

A beneficiary designation is irrevocable when the WBG pension becomes payable.

---

96. *Id.* Article 4.2(b) *stating* that a surviving spouse or domestic partner will receive certain benefits and if there is no surviving spouse or domestic partner at the time of death then the designated beneficiary will receive the benefits described herein.

97. *Id.* Article 4.2(c).

3.3.3 Death Without a Surviving Spouse or Domestic Partner

If the participant dies without a surviving spouse or domestic partner while still an employee of the WBG, the participant's beneficiaries will receive a lump sum calculated as follows:[98]

Two times the participant's final net salary

plus

8 percent of the participant's highest average net salary *times* the number of years of service with the WBG

plus

the participant's cash balance account valued as of the first day of the month after the participant's death

plus

the termination grant that would have been payable to the participant valued as of the date of the participant's death (if applicable)

If a participant dies without a surviving spouse or domestic partner after leaving the employ of the WBG but before commencing their pension benefits, then the participant's beneficiaries would receive a lump sum calculated as follows:[99]

8 percent of the participant's highest average net salary *times* the number of years of service with the WBG

plus

the participant's cash balance account valued as of the first day of the month after the participant's death

plus

the termination grant that would have been payable to the participant valued as of the date of the participant's death (if applicable)

98. *Id.* Article 4.4(c).
99. *Id.* Article 4.4(e).

The portion of the lump-sum death benefit that is based on the termination grant (when the participant has deferred payment of their pension benefits) is eligible for cost-of-living increases.[100]

3.4 Survivor Pensions

These optional survivor benefits are the benefits potentially available to a former spouse of a WBG employee. They must be secured by election, and reference to them in a court order to divide the SRP benefits will not be enforced by the WBG.

3.4.1 Survivor Pension Available for Former Spouse

In a divorce, a former spouse may receive a former spouse survivor pension up to 100 percent of the total employee pension payment. In order to pay such a benefit, the WBG will reduce the payment made during the participant's lifetime.

PRACTICE TIP

The maximum survivor pension for WBG is 100 percent of the employee's monthly pension payment.

If the participant began participation in the Net Plan prior to December 31, 2015, then the payment to the former spouse during the participant's lifetime will be reduced to provide for the survivor pension. If the participant began participation in the Net Plan on or after January 1, 2016, the participant's pension will be reduced to provide for the former spouse's survivor pension if the age difference between the parties is less than five years. If it is more than five years, then both the participant and the former spouse's payments during the participant's lifetime will be reduced.[101] See Appendix 2 for the full chart of the pension reduction factors.

---

100. *Id.* Article 8.3(b).
101. *Id.*

PRACTICE TIP

The plan will not shift the reduction to provide the former spouse's survivor benefit per a court order. As such, if the parties wish to shift the cost, the parties will need to enter an order at the time of the divorce to secure the benefits and then amend the order at the time of the participant's retirement to shift the reduction to provide for the former spouse's survivor benefit accordingly. If the participant is close to retirement, they may be able to obtain calculations from the WBG prior to the divorce.

A word of warning: if the participant remarries before retirement, the participant will have the option to increase the survivor benefit payable to their subsequent spouse. If they increase the benefit to the subsequent spouse to be 100 percent of their pension benefit, then there will not be a survivor benefit payable to a former spouse, regardless of the agreement.

If the participant is not yet retired, they must submit an election to the benefits administrator at any time prior to beginning to commence benefits.[102] In addition, posthumous elections will not be accepted; the election must be on file prior to death of the participant. The reduction to the pension would begin as of the first payment. If the participant is not yet retired, the election can be revoked at any time prior to the participant's death, or the date the participant begins to receive their pension benefit.[103]

If the participant is already retired, they must submit an election to the benefit administrator within 180 days of the date of divorce.[104] The election will become effective one year after the date of divorce and cannot be revoked once effective.[105] The reduction to the pension will begin once the election is effective.[106]

---

102. *Id.* Article 11.3(b).
103. *Id.* Article 11.3(b)(ii).
104. *Id.* Article 11.3(a).
105. *Id.*
106. *Id.*

PRACTICE TIP

An important note here: the participant's pension cannot be reduced to less than half of the unreduced pension during the participant's lifetime due to all reductions—including all survivor pensions.[107] In addition, the total of the survivor pensions payable must be equal or less than the reduced amount payable to the participant during their lifetime.[108] In the event a person to receive a survivor pension dies before the participant, the election is moot, and benefits are paid as if no election had been made.[109]

3.5 Refunds and Transfers to Other Institutions

The World Bank has agreements with the United Nations Joint Staff Pension Fund (UNJSPF), the IMF, and the Inter-American Development Bank (IDB) to transfer a participant's interest in their pension system in the event of a change of employment.[110] If a World Bank participant wants to transfer interest to a different system, they must meet the eligibility requirements and make an election within 180 days if coming from the IMF, or within six months if coming from the UNJSPF or the IDB.[111] Transfers are not automatic.

3.5.1 Transfers Between the UNJSPF and the World Bank SRP

3.5.1.1 Transfer from the World Bank SRP to the UNJSPF

If a World Bank SRP participant becomes a participant in the UNJSPF and wants to transfer their World Bank pension interest to the UNJSPF, the World Bank SRP will pay a sum to the UNJSPF representing the financial interest. After such payment, the participant

107. *Id.* Article 11.3(a)(ii).
108. *Id.*
109. *Id.* Article 11.3(a)(iii).
110. G00203 Summary of Benefits Applicable to Headquarters-based Open and Term Staff. World Bank HR Operations Publication (June 29, 2020).
111. *Id.*

will no longer have an interest in the World Bank SRP. However, the participant will have gained time in the UNJSPF prior to their actual starting date of participation in the UNJSPF.

The amount of the payment from the World Bank SRP to the UNJSPF is the equivalent of the World Bank SRP withdrawal benefit to the participant, the actuarial equivalent of all World Bank SRP benefits that would have been payable in an annuity, plus 15 percent of the sum of these two amounts.[112]

The amount of contributory service the participant is credited with in the UNJSPF is actuarily calculated by the UNJSPF based on the payment received from the World Bank SRP.[113]

Since the amount of time the participant will have credited to them in the UNJSPF will be actuarily calculated, it is important to obtain from the participant or the UNJSPF directly how much time the participant was credited with. The reason for this is that a straight marital share fraction[114] will not divide the pension as intended, especially if premarital time was transferred, or post-divorce time will be accrued. For example, if the participant is credited with less time in the UNJSPF than the participant actually contributed to the World Bank SRP, then a straight marital share fraction would incorrectly assign some premarital time to the marital time.

PRACTICE TIP

Transfers between institutions can muddle the concepts of marital and nonmarital. When a transfer may have occurred, make sure to tread lightly and, if necessary, consult an expert.

---

112. Agreement of the transfer of pension rights of participants in the United Nations Joint Staff Pension Fund and of participants in the World Bank Group Staff Retirement Plan.

113. *Id.*

114. "Marital share fraction" in this pension context means a fraction in which the numerator is the total number of months during the marriage that the participant contributed to the plan, and the denominator is the total number of months the participant contributed to the plan at the time of retirement.

How to solve this is to learn how much time the UNJSPF credited the participant from the time transferred from the World Bank SRP. Then, divide the UNJSPF time transferred by the amount of time actually spent contributing to the World Bank SRP. This resulting percent should then be multiplied by the time credited in the UNJSPF to determine the marital amount of time transferred to the UNJSPF. In any agreement, court order, or proposed judgment, the numerator of the marital share fraction should be described as the actual number of months,[115] rather than "the number of months the participant contributed to the plan during the parties' marriage." The reason for this is because the UNJSPF (or any pension receiving a transfer) will not look into whether time transferred over was actuarily adjusted, or if it was transferred on a one-to-one basis. The plans will simply look at the plan entry and termination dates and see where they overlap with the dates of marriage and divorce. An agreement should include a description of the math, to serve as a confirmation of how the numerator of the marital share fraction was calculated. A final order to the plan should describe the numerator as the defined number for best clarity.

3.5.1.2 Transfers from the UNJSPF to the World Bank SRP

Upon the UNJSPF participant's election to transfer their benefits to the World Bank SRP, they will no longer be eligible to receive benefits from the UNJSPF.[116] In addition, the participant may not have received any retirement benefits from the UNJSPF prior to their election to transfer their interest to the World Bank SRP.[117] In other words, if the participant has received any retirement benefits from the UNJSPF, they are ineligible to transfer their benefits to the WBG SRP.

To effectuate the transfer, the UNJSPF will pay to the World Bank SRP the larger of (1) the actuarial value of the participant's accrued UNJSPF interest based on the contributory service and final average remuneration as of the date participation in the UNJSPF ceased; or (2) the withdrawal settlement amount the participant would have

115. Months, days, years, whichever unit of time the plan prefers to use.

116. Agreement of the transfer of pension rights of participants in the United Nations Joint Staff Pension Fund and of participants in the World Bank Group Staff Retirement Plan.

117. *Id.*

received had they made such election upon terminating service with the employing member organization.[118]

The World Bank SRP will create a second cash balance account for the participant to receive the funds from the UNJSPF.[119] This cash balance account will not be considered or eligible for the tax supplement payment payable from the World Bank to the participant.[120] Since the payment from the UNJSPF is kept separate from the contributions from the participant to the World Bank SRP, the benefits payable from the SRP from the defined benefit and first cash balance accounts (which are created and maintained based on the participant's service with the World Bank and member organizations) are based only on the participant's creditable service with the World Bank (and member organizations) and the participant's final average remuneration from their employment with the World Bank and member organizations. The participant's transferred service time from the UNJSPF will count toward the participant's eligibility for retirement, however.[121]

3.6 Division in Divorce

3.6.1 How to Divide the Employee Pension

The agreement and order should describe the payment to the former spouse as a dollar amount, percent, or formula.[122] Any formula expressing the participant's creditable service in the World Bank plan should express their service in terms of days, rather than months or years.[123]

The order should also state whether the former spouse is to receive a share of the monthly payments, any lump sum payments, or both.[124] With respect to any lump sum awarded to the former spouse, the percent, formula, or dollar amount can be described as of a certain date. If including a date certain, then a specific rate of return can

118. *Id.*
119. *Id.*
120. *Id.* Article 3.
121. *Id.*
122. World Bank Model Order and Instructions.
123. *Id.*
124. *Id.*

be included. The World Bank will not calculate generic "gains and losses" on the specified amount, but the specific rate of return can be tied to a fund in which the cash balance portion can be invested, such as the Real 3 Investment Index which is the World Bank's most conservative fund.

PRACTICE TIP

The World Bank will not calculate generic earnings, gains, and losses on a CB lump-sum payment.

Since the payment obligation per the World Bank is "a legal obligation arising from a marital relationship to support [a former spouse]," the amount of the pension and annuity payments to the former spouse can be changed at any time.[125] To change the amount payable to the former spouse, the parties would have to submit an Amended Order for Spousal Support to the WBG.

It is interesting that an appellant once tried to argue that due to the World Bank's privileges and immunities that the World Bank pension must be divided via a cash lump-sum payment based on the present value of the pension as of the date of divorce.[126] The court expressly rejected this argument and ordered an "if, as, and when" type division of the pension.[127]

3.6.2 How to Divide Former Spouse Survivor Pension

The order may require the participant to designate the former spouse as beneficiary of the survivor benefit.[128] However, it is the beneficiary designation on file with the World Bank at the time of the participant's death that governs, therefore, any such language in the order is not enforceable against the World Bank.[129] In the event that the participant remarries at any time before receiving benefits from the

125. WBG SRP, Article 7.2(c).
126. De Liedekerke v. De Liedekerke, 635 A.2d 339, 341 (D.C. App. 1993).
127. *Id.*
128. World Bank Model Order and Instructions.
129. *Id.*

pension, the spouse at the time benefits begin (or in the case of the participant's death before retirement) will be the "surviving spouse" and have to consent to the beneficiary designation to the former spouse.[130]

If the participant elects to decrease their pension payment to allow for a former spouse's survivor pension, that must also be secured by the participant's election thereof on a designation form submitted to the WBG. See Section 3.3.1 for additional information.

3.6.3 How to Allocate Cost of Survivor Pension

The cost of the survivor pension cannot be shifted via simple language in the court order directing the WBG to do so. This is because the survivor pension is governed by a designation form and not the court order. The plan states that the reduction to the annuity during the participant's lifetime to provide for this additional survivor pension for the former spouse must come from the participant's share of the pension. However, the WBG has published its reduction factor charts, so the amount of the reduction can be estimated. Therefore, the formula to determine the former spouse's share of the benefit can be modified to absorb the reduction. See Appendix 2 herein.

3.6.4 Treatment of Post-Divorce Salary Adjustments

With respect to any amount not commuted, the World Bank will not accept orders applying the former spouse's percentage of benefits to any amount *other than* the final monthly benefit paid to the participant.[131] Therefore, the parties cannot request that the World Bank alter their calculation of the participant's benefit for the purposes of determining the former spouse's benefit.[132] The parties can, however, request estimates of the benefit during the negotiations to help approximate the benefit receivable at that time as a dollar amount. They could then describe their detailed calculations within the separation agreement and simply describe the former spouse's share as a dollar amount in the order, rather than a percentage, in order to circumvent the World Bank's rule here.

---

130. *Id.*
131. Experience, case specific.
132. *Id.*

3.6.5 Orders

While the World Bank is not required to accept a state court order pursuant to their privileges and immunities, they have made one clear exception to accept orders for spousal support as a means to divide the employee's pension benefit.[133] The World Bank requires the following information to be included in any order:

1. That it be called an Order for Spousal Support and include a statement that the participant has an obligation arising from a marital relationship to support their former or legally separated spouse, and that the participant is ordered to make such payment from the benefits received from the plan.[134] If the order requires the World Bank to make the payments on behalf of the participant, the order will be rejected.[135]

PRACTICE TIP

The order for the World Bank must be called an Order for Spousal Support. Any title referring to a division of retirement interests or a property division will be rejected.

2. The amount of the support must be clear. If it is in any way vague, the order will be rejected. The World Bank does not interpret orders or the underlying agreements.[136]
3. The currency of the payment to the former spouse should be included in the order.[137] The default currency is the same as the participant's currency; however, the former spouse could also receive their payment in the currency of the country in which they reside.[138]

---

133. World Bank Model and Instructions.

134. *Id.*

135. *Id.* In Maryland, the courts have accepted that the order being sent to the World Bank must be titled for Spousal Support but continue to treat the payments as retirement benefits in the division of marital property. Abdullahi v. Zanini, 241 Ad. App. 372, 418–24, 211, A.3d 510 (Md. App. 2019).

136. World Bank Model and Instructions.

137. *Id.*

138. *Id.*

4. Information necessary to identify the parties. This includes the current address, date of birth, and social security number (if applicable) for each party.[139] This information may be submitted in a separate letter or addendum accompanying the order so that it is not a part of the public court order, and we recommend doing so.

In addition, the order may have provisions regarding the following, which the World Bank will honor:

1. Cost of living adjustments. If the order is silent, then they will not be applied to the former spouse's benefit. So, if the parties agree to divide them, then it must be stated explicitly in the order.[140]
2. Ability for the former spouse to obtain information regarding the participant's benefit and retirement eligibility. Once the parties divorce, the World Bank will require the participant's approval to provide any such information to the former spouse.[141] However, former spouses may want this information for retirement planning purposes. Therefore, the World Bank will accept language in the order that restores the former spouse's access to information in this limited capacity.[142] Without this provision in the order, the former spouse would have to request the information from the participant who would not have an obligation to provide it.

Finally, the order may also include provisions regarding the following, which the World Bank will *not* honor, but such terms will not cause the order to be rejected:

1. Election of death benefits and designation of beneficiary. The World Bank is clear that the beneficiary designation form governs this benefit.[143]

---

139. *Id.*

140. *Id.*

141. *See* Section 3.9.7 herein (Information Requests directed to the World Bank).

142. World Bank Model and Instructions.

143. *Id.*; Domestic Relations Manual. In this author's experience, in a review of draft orders by the World Bank, they request any such provisions be deleted.

2. Requiring the participant to take the pension benefits in any particular form or at any particular time (i.e., take early retirement or take a certain amount of the cash balance benefit as a lump sum).[144]
3. Require the participant to take any steps regarding the life insurance benefit.[145]

With respect to these provisions that the World Bank will not honor, the attorneys should ensure that these provisions are in some other court order or written document so that they are enforceable against the participant should the participant fail to comply. Options for such other writing includes a separate consent order or incorporating and/or merging the parties' separation agreement into the divorce decree.

Other considerations if the parties agree to such terms are what will be the remedy should the participant fail to comply. For example, what if the participant was supposed to take a large lump sum at retirement and now does not have the cash available to make a direct payment to the former spouse? This situation could easily turn into prolonged litigation following a period of discovery to determine the best outcome. Alternatively, the parties could agree in advance to a remedy.

Agreements about how the participant will take benefits at retirement are difficult to enforce because the World Bank will not enforce them. There are many scenarios like the one just outlined in the preceding paragraph where the participant could breach the agreement, and the former spouse is left with only court remedies.

In addition, the timing of the submission of the Order for Spousal Support and any election for an optional survivor pension for the former spouse is important. Take for example the repercussions of the participant's decision to take the benefit as a lump sum or annuity. As described earlier, if the participant elects to receive both the CB and DB components as lump sums, then there will not be a survivor benefit payable. If the Order for Spousal Support is not submitted to the WBG prior to the lump-sum payment to the participant, the former spouse will not receive any direct payment from the WBG. In order

144. World Bank Model and Instructions.

145. *Id.*

to secure their share of the pension *and* funds in place of the survivor benefit, the former spouse will have to chase down the participant and get direct payment from the participant. If the participant has already spent the funds, it may be extremely difficult to recover them from the participant. Moreover, since the payment amount will likely be quite substantial, the former spouse will want to consult with a financial planner to determine how best to invest their share of the funds to replicate any survivor pension they otherwise would have received from the WBG (had the participant elected to receive an annuity).

3.6.6 Additional Forms

In addition to the Order for Spousal Support, the participant is to write an acknowledgment to the plan administrator describing the obligation and summarizing the benefits to be provided to the former spouse.[146] The World Bank provides sample language for this acknowledgment (see Figure 3.1).[147]

THE WORLD BANK/IFC/M.I.G.A.
OFFICE MEMORANDUM

DATE:

TO: Plan Administrator, Staff Retirement Plan

FROM:

EXTENSION:

SUBJECT: **Acknowledgement of Legal Obligation to Pay Spousal Support (Net Plan)**

Pursuant to Section 5A.2(c) of the Staff Retirement Plan, I hereby acknowledge that I am under a legal obligation to provide Spousal Support to my former spouse or legally separated spouse. This obligation is evidenced and/or imposed by the attached certified order of a court of competent jurisdiction. If, as and when my benefits become payable, I acknowledge that $_______ [or ____%] of the benefit payable to me under Articles 3A and 4A of the Staff Retirement Plan shall be paid directly to ______________ who is my former spouse or legally separated spouse to whom I have a legal obligation of support arising from the marital relationship.

____

[Signature]

Figure 3.1 World Bank sample acknowledgment of legal obligation to pay spousal support

146. *Id.*
147. *Id.*

In the event that the participant does not execute such acknowledgment within 30 days of the order for spousal support being entered by the court, the former spouse may file a similar document requesting payment from the plan administrator.

3.6.7 Contact Information[148]

World Bank Group headquarters is located at 1818 H Street, NW, Washington, D.C. 20443, and their main phone number is 202-473-1000. If a participant or soon-to-be former spouse needs to contact HR operations for any information regarding the participant's benefits, they can send an email to: hroperations@worldbank.org, call 202-473-2222, or fax 202-522-2150. Alternatively, HR operations can be reached via mail at: World Bank HR Operations, MSN G2-202, P.O. Box 1420, Landover, Maryland 20785.

If looking for information regarding the pension in particular, the pension administration can be reached at: The World Bank, MSN C6-605, 1818 H Street, NW, Washington, D.C. 20433, 1pension@worldbank.org, phone 202-458-2977 or fax 202-522-1723. The participant can also log in to view their benefits online at www.pension.worldbank.org.

3.7 Remarriage of Employee

If the employee/participant remarries while still employed with the WBG, the employee may elect to provide an increased survivor benefit for their subsequent spouse. In such an event, the amount of the survivor benefit available for the former spouse would be decreased. See Section 3.3.1 herein. In addition, such additional survivor benefit for the subsequent spouse would cause a reduction in the employee's pension benefits during the employee's lifetime, thereby reducing any such payments to the former spouse. It is important to address these possibilities in any agreement so that if they come to pass, the former spouse is not left with less than bargained for in the agreement.

148. All contact information is current as of the date of publishing.

3.8 Remarriage of Former Spouse

Since the orders to the WBG are titled as Spousal Support orders, they must address how the payments to the Former Spouse will be impacted, if at all, by the former spouse's remarriage. For example, payments of the employee's pension benefit or survivor annuity could terminate upon the former spouse's remarriage, or the benefit payments to the former spouse could remain the same in such event.

3.9 Savings Plan/401(k)

3.9.1 Overview

The World Bank Group headquarters 401(k) plan (WBG 401(k) plan) was established on July 1, 2009. Participation is voluntary. An employee may participate if they are a regular, open-ended, term, extended term consultant, or extended term temporary staff. In addition, an executive director, senior advisor or advisor to an executive director, or the president are also eligible to participate. It provides staff with flexibility to supplement their retirement savings with more flexible distribution options than the pension plan. The WBG 401(k) plan enables eligible staff to make contributions to a tax-deferred savings plan, regardless of nationality. The WBG 401(k) plan offers three types of accounts: a traditional pretax account, a Roth account, and after-tax account, which allows the employee to contribute above the prescribed limits for the pretax and Roth accounts. The World Bank does not contribute to the 401(k) plan. The payout from the WBG 401(k) plan can be made in a lump sum or installments. There is no tax supplement on benefit distributions from the WBG 401(k) plan.

The WBG 401(k) plan is currently administered by Wells Fargo, and account statements can be accessed at www.wellsfargo.com. The account statements are generated quarterly and contain other valuable information such as date of birth, date of hire, participation date, marital status and beneficiary designation.

The WBG 401(k) plan offers a range of investment options such as cash-equivalents, bonds, domestic and international stocks, and target date funds. The account balance is maintained in U.S. dollars. If the employee is not paid in U.S. dollars, the contributions will be converted from the employee's salary currency to U.S. dollars based on the market exchange rate on the date that funds are transferred to the plan trustee.

3.9.2 Plan Limits and Taxation

Annual contributions to the 401(k) plan are subject to the limitations imposed by the IRS, however there are no income limitations.

Traditional Pretax Account. For traditional pretax accounts, funds are deposited on a pretax basis, meaning they are not taxed as income in that year. This results in a relatively immediate tax savings. However, the funds are taxed as income upon withdrawal. The contribution limit was $23,000 as of 2024, plus employees 50 and over can make up to an additional $7,500 "catch-up contribution" each year.

Roth Account. For the Roth savings, the funds contributed to the account have already been taxed as income to the employee (as applicable), meaning there is no tax savings in the current year. However, the income in retirement will not be taxed. Also, withdrawals can be made from the Roth 401(k) tax-free, and without incurring a 10 percent early withdrawal penalty after age 59½ if the account has been open for at least five years. There are no income limitations.

Required Minimum Distributions. The employee will be obligated to take required minimum distributions (RMDs) from their WBG 401(k) upon reaching age 73 even if still employed.[149] However, they can avoid RMDs from a Roth 401(k) by rolling over the money into a Roth IRA, which doesn't require minimum distributions.

The following items should be addressed in a domestic relations order (DRO). Social security numbers and dates of birth are typically included in the cover letter to the plan.

- **Party names and addresses**
- **Official name of plan**
- **Amount of alternate payee's benefits.** Stated either as a specific dollar amount or percentage.

---

149. The Secure 2.0 Act raised the age that account owners must begin taking RMDs. In 2023, the age at which account owners must start taking required minimum distributions went up from age 72 to age 73, so individuals born in 1951 must receive their first required minimum distribution by April 1, 2025.

- **Commencement date.** Language that allows the alternate payee the right to elect to commence benefits as soon as administratively feasible following the date that the QDRO is approved.
- **Lump-sum payment.** State that the alternate payee is to receive their share in a lump sum.
- **Survivorship rights.** The extent of any survivorship rights to which the alternate payee will be entitled in the event of the participant's death.
- **Earnings/gains/losses.** If you wish to provide the alternate payee with earnings, gains, and losses on their share, the DRO should so state. If silent, the plan administrator will automatically apply earnings, gains, and losses from the effective date of the assignment to the distribution date.
- **Pro-rata allocation of investments.** If the DRO is silent, the alternate payee's share of the benefits, whether a fixed dollar amount or a percentage, shall be allocated on a "pro-rata" basis among all of the participant's sub-accounts and/or investment funds.
- **Loans.** Unless otherwise specified in the QDRO, the alternate payee's share of the benefits will be calculated "*with regard to*" any outstanding loan balance such that the outstanding loan balance will be subtracted from the account balance when calculating the alternate payee's share.[150] Alternatively, you may specify that the alternate payee's share be calculated "*without regard to*" any loans. If you include this language, the alternate payee's share of the benefits will be based on the participant's total vested account balance as if no loans were ever taken.

---

150. QDRO Consultants provides this example:

> John had a total account balance under the plan of $100,000. However, he took a loan for $20,000 just prior to his divorce. A QDRO is submitted shortly after their divorce that awards 50 percent of John's total account balance as of his date of divorce to his former spouse, Mary. If the QDRO is otherwise silent regarding the disposition of the outstanding loan balance, the QDRO will be interpreted to provide Mary with $40,000 (i.e., half of the remaining $80,000 after the loan balance is subtracted).

PRACTICE TIP

"Earnings, gains, and losses" is the phrase used to describe the investment experience of the funds within a defined contribution account such as a 401(k). In dividing a 401(k), the parties have the option of including earnings, gains, and losses on the amount to be transferred, or not. One must select a valuation date from which to apply the earnings gains and losses.

Division of the earnings, gains, and losses protects against surprises in the market.

By way of example, say Spouse A is to receive 50 percent of Spouse B's old 401(k) as of December 31, 2023, with earnings, gains, and losses applied thereon (Spouse B and the employer are no longer contributing to the 401(k)). At the time, $100,000 was in the account. Due to market fluctuations, at the time the account was to be divided, only $80,000 was in the account. Therefore, each party received $40,000 upon division.

Assume the same facts as preceding, but this time with no earnings, gains, and losses applied. Spouse A will receive $50,000 and Spouse B will retain $30,000.

Continue to assume the same facts, but this time due to market fluctuations only $40,000 remained in the account at the time it was to be divided. Without earnings, gains, and losses Spouse A would receive all $40,000 (even though Spouse A should have received $50,000), Spouse B would be left with $0, and the plan would consider its obligation satisfied.

For this reason, we recommend always including earnings, gains, and losses in a defined contribution division.

3.9.3 Submitting the DRO

A private company called QDRO Consultants is the designated review agent of the WBG 401(k) plan for purposes of receiving, processing, accepting, or rejecting QDROs. Because the WBG 401(k) plan is an

ERISA covered, qualified plan, only a DRO is appropriate to divide the account. QDRO Consultants will review draft orders for preapproval. The drafts may be submitted through their website (qdros .com/submit), and they will also answer questions. There is a one-time fee of $400 to review the orders, which will be drawn from the participant's account.

PRACTICE TIP

What is ERISA? What does it mean to be a qualified plan?

ERISA is the Employee Retirement Income Security Act, a federal statute passed in 1974 and revised periodically since then. The main purpose of ERISA is to protect employees' retirement savings in plans provided by employers by providing minimum standards for the plan fiduciaries. Plans that are regulated by ERISA are called "qualified" plans. Most importantly, qualified plans are required to be divisible by QDRO. This requirement means that it is possible to transfer a share of a qualified plan from one spouse to another as a part of the divorce proceedings. ERISA also provides minimum requirements for a participant to take out a loan from a retirement plan or protect a spouse's interest in the survivor benefit during the marriage. These protections mean that during the marriage, the retirement account is protected from being disbursed without spousal consent, and the spouse must approve of someone else getting the survivor benefit. Once the divorce is final, those protections end.

If you submit a draft DRO for preapproval, there will be a hold placed on the participant's benefit meaning that no withdrawals or transfers can be affected until the hold is released. A hold shall be in effect for six months; however, it can be extended under the discretion of the plan administrator if it is clear that a QDRO is still being pursued. When submitting a DRO for final approval, you must ensure the order is signed by a judge and also enclose the Personal Information Addendum form (Figure 3.2).

DO NOT FILE WITH COURT

QDRO Consultants

your partner in QDRO and QMCSO services

Personal Information Addendum

This form is provided to ensure that your personal information is protected. This addendum should not be filed with the court. Instead, this addendum should be included with the draft or executed order you submit for review. **Please note that this information is required to qualify and process a qualified domestic relations order (QDRO).**

Plan Sponsor:

PARTICIPANT	ALTERNATE PAYEE
Name	**Name**
Address (Street, City, State, Zip)	**Address (Street, City, State, Zip)**
Social Security Number	**Social Security Number**
Date of Birth	**Date of Birth**
Email Address	**Email Address**
	Relationship to Participant

SUBMITTING PARTY

Name

Phone	**Date**	**Email Address**

DISCLAIMER: This form should be submitted securely through our website. Go to https://qdros.com/submit/ to upload.

Last Revised 8/10/22

DO NOT FILE WITH COURT

Figure 3.2 Example of a personal information addendum form

PRACTICE TIP

All pertinent documentation, requests for DRO review, and requests for QDRO information or model orders should be addressed to:

QDRO Consultants Co.
3071 Pearl Road
Medina, OH 44256
Attn: The World Bank QDRO Compliance Team
Phone: (800) 527-8481
Fax: (330) 722-2735

Upon receipt of a purported DRO, QDRO Consultants Co. will notify the parties regarding the order's approval as a QDRO and will send an "interpretation letter" to all parties and attorneys.

3.10 Other Benefits

3.10.1 Health Benefits

The World Bank Group sponsors a health, vision, and dental insurance program called the Medical Insurance Plan (MIP).[151] Coverage is optional and commences as of the first day of employment so long as the employee completes enrollment within 60 days of their employment beginning.[152] The World Bank pays a part of the monthly premiums, and the employee's share of the premium is deducted from their pay each pay period.[153]

Former spouses can continue their coverage under the MIP under the MIP continuation program for up to 36 months, subject to multiple conditions.[154] The conditions are fully explained in the Domestic Relations and World Bank Group Families: An Information Package

---

151. G00203 Summary of Benefits Applicable to Headquarters-based Open and Term Staff, *supra* note 110.

152. *Id.*

153. *Id.*

154. Domestic Relations and World Bank Group Families: An Information Package for World Bank Group Employees, Spouses, Lawyers, and Advocates, Appendix D (Version 8, Sept. 12, 2019).

for World Bank Group Employees, Spouses, Lawyers, and Advocates, Appendix D (Version 8, Sept. 12, 2019),[155] however, a few conditions are specifically worth noting here.

- The application for MIP continuation must be made within 60 days of the loss event (i.e., divorce) or it will not be available. Coverage for the former spouse automatically ends on the last day of the month in which the divorce is final.
- The former spouse will be responsible for the full premium cost—there is no amount paid by the World Bank Group.
- MIP continuation must be for the same plan.
- MIP continuation can only be increased if the person is pregnant while applying, in which case it can be increased to cover the child. If the person becomes pregnant while the coverage has already started, the child is covered for 60 days under the mother's coverage only.

In addition, the employee is required to provide the former spouse with a MIP continuation application.[156] The World Bank Group HR Service Center will, however, provide applications upon request if needed.[157]

PRACTICE TIP

The application for MIP continuation must be made within 60 days of the loss event (i.e., divorce) or it will not be available. Coverage for the former spouse automatically ends on the last day of the month in which the divorce is final.[158]

3.10.2 Life Insurance

The life insurance policy paid for by the World Bank Group is equal to the employee's annual net salary.[159] Employees can pay for optional

155. *See* Appendix 4 in this book.
156. *Id.*
157. *Id.*
158. *Id.*
159. Domestic Relations and World Bank Group Families, *supra* note 154, at Section 2.16.

additional coverage up to six times their annual net salary.[160] The employee can change their beneficiary at any time, and the beneficiary form on file at the time of the employee's death is controlling.[161]

PRACTICE TIP

World Bank insurance policies can be irrevocably assigned.

Ownership of the policy is assignable.[162] If assigned, the new policy owner can change the policy coverage and beneficiary, and the employee no longer has such authority.[163] Counsel will need to determine if their state courts have the authority to order an assignment of life insurance policies.[164]

Parties can also purchase dependent life insurance for the spouse and eligible children.[165] The employee is automatically the beneficiary of the policy.[166] Coverage is either standard ($20,000 for a spouse and $8,000 for a child) or high ($50,000 for a spouse and $10,000 for a child).[167]

3.10.3 Accidental Death and Dismemberment Insurance

WBG staff are automatically enrolled in the basic accidental death and dismemberment insurance coverage, which is fully paid by the WBG.[168] The benefit amount is 300 percent of the employee's net

160. *Id.*

161. *Id.* Section 2.17.

162. *Id.* Section 2.18.

163. *Id.*

164. Certain states have published cases regarding the assignability of life insurance policies. *See* Sedarous v. Sedarous, 285 N.J. Super. 316, 666 A.2d 1362 (App. Div. 1995); Kidd v. Pritzel, 821 S.W.2d 566 (Mo. App. 1991); Roberts v. Roberts, 560 S.W.2d 438 (Tex. Ct. Civ. App. 1977); Metropolitan Life Ins. Co. v. Christ, 979 F.2d 575 (7th Cir. 1992) Dean v. Johnson, 881 F.2d 948 (10th Cir. 1989); Metropolitan Life Ins. Co. v. Thompson, 968 F. Supp. 312 (S.D. Miss. 1997); Metropolitan Life Ins. Co. v. Potter, 533 So. 2d 589 (1988).

165. Domestic Relations and World Bank Group Families, *supra* note 154, at Section 2.19.

166. *Id.*

167. *Id.*

168. WBG Benefits Overview, Headquarter Staff (June 2018).

salary for the employee; 150 percent of the employee's net salary for the domestic partner/spouse, and 75 percent of the employee's net salary for each child.[169]

An employee can purchase additional, optional coverage at the employee's full expense if desired.[170] Premium amounts and coverage amounts will vary based on the amount selected by the employee.

3.10.4 Benefits for Families Stationed Overseas

Families stationed overseas have many of the same benefits as those stationed within the United States; however, the program or the provider of the benefits may be different. Additional benefits that are available to overseas staff include loans for settling into the new duty location, housing loans, and emergency loans.[171] It is important to confer with your client to see if there are additional benefits that are divisible or impacted due to the divorce.

3.10.5 Education Benefits/Mobility Premium

3.10.5.1 Education Benefits

A World Bank employee may be eligible for education benefits. Such benefits include (but are not limited to) tuition, room and board (if the educational institution is outside of the employee's duty station country), application fees, mandatory computer software purchases, diploma fees, exam fees (PSAT, SAT, GRE, AP TOEFL, baccalaureate), graduation fees, and lab fees.[172] Expenses that are not included are expenses such as activity or sports fees, before- and after-care expenses, early arrival or late stay fees, clothes/uniforms, fitness center, field trips, musical instruments, PTA dues, and data connectivity fees.[173] See Appendix 3 for the full list of covered and noncovered expenses.

If the employee is eligible for such benefits, the benefits are for children only, not the employee, spouse, or third party. Generally,

---

169. *Id.*

170. *Id.*

171. WBG Benefits Overview, Country Staff (May 2018).

172. https://www.worldbank.org/en/about/unit/human-resources/education-benefits (last visited May 1, 2025).

173. *Id.*

an employee is eligible for education benefits when they are hired to a regular, fixed term, open-ended, or executive director's assistant appointment on or before June 30, 1999, and are appointed to an international recruitment.[174] The employee must not be a citizen or permanent resident of the country in which they are serving, nor could they have been a citizen or permanent resident of such county within the 12 months preceding their appointment to such country.[175] To find out if the participant in your case is eligible or for more specific information, the participant or spouse should request such information from the World Bank.

Benefits may begin for the academic year in which the child turns five years old.[176] If the child has a summer birthday, then the benefits begin for the academic year following the child's fifth birthday.[177] Education benefits will end in the academic year in which the child turns 24 years old (for employees on assignment effective before January 1, 2016).[178] For employees on assignment effective on or after January 1, 2016, benefits can continue until the academic year in which the child turns 22 years old, completes four years of qualifying tertiary education, or completes their first university/college degree, whichever first occurs.[179]

In addition, eligibility for the education benefit ceases after five years for employees on indefinite appointments.[180]

---

174. World Bank Staff Rule 6.14, Section 3.01–3.03 (Dec. 8, 2020). More specific regulations regarding eligibility based on employment type is based on the time of hire.

175. *Id.*

176. *Id.* Section 3.09.

177. *Id.*

178. *Id.* Section 3.10. Benefits may continue for one additional academic year in the event the child must leave school to participate in a compulsory military service lasting six months or more. Benefits may end sooner if the employee's eligible assignment terminates.

179. *Id.* Section 3.11. Benefits may continue until the academic year in which the child reaches age 23 in the event the child must leave school to participate in compulsory military service lasting six months or more, assuming the other two terminating events have not been satisfied. *Id.*

180. *Id.*

Qualifying education includes full-time[181] attendance at a recognized institution for pre-primary, primary, or secondary education.[182] If attending such school in the same country as the employee's duty country, the education benefits can also include language instruction in the employee's or spouse's primary language, if that is not the language of the duty country.[183] Education benefits can also include 12 months of language instruction in the language of the duty country, if that is not the language of the employee or spouse.[184] If the child is attending public school, then the benefits can also include instruction in academic subjects necessary for the child to return to school in their home country.[185]

Education benefits also apply to college or university expenses, so long as the courses lead to a degree or diploma.[186] However, if the host duty station is in Washington, D.C., or New York, then the education institution must be outside the United States.[187]

Distance learning is also covered in the education benefits so long as the distance learning is full-time primary, secondary, or university study leading to a degree, and is not supplemental to some other full-time degree program.[188]

The amount of benefits available is generally up to 100 percent of qualifying pre-primary, primary, and secondary education, expenses and up to 75 percent of qualifying tertiary education expenses, up to the maximum allowed.[189]

3.10.5.2 Home Country Travel

Certain employees in positions subject to international recruitment on open-ended, term, or executive director advisor roles, may

---

181. At least three hours per day, five days per week. *Id.* Section 4.01.
182. *Id.*
183. *Id.*
184. *Id.*
185. *Id.*
186. *Id.* Section 4.01.
187. *Id.* Section 4.02.
188. *Id.* Sections 4.01–402.
189. *Id.* Section 5.01. There are different maximums for the Northern and Southern Hemispheres, and manager approval required for instruction in languages. *Id.*

be eligible to receive a home country travel benefit.[190] This is only for international positions; U.S. positions receive the mobility premium. The travel grant available as part of the home country travel benefit is the amount of the most direct and cost-effective, economy class round trip travel between the duty station and the employee's home country.[191] This amount is determined by the travel office and reviewed twice per year.[192]

The employee and immediate family members are also eligible for a home country grant in the amount of $1,600 for the employee and $800 for each spouse and eligible, dependent child.[193] The purpose of this grant is to help defray additional travel costs such as visas, taxis, and so on.[194] After divorce, the former spouse is no longer eligible for this benefit.

3.10.5.3 Mobility Premium

The mobility premium is paid to a World Bank employee on an open-ended or term appointment at a grade level GF or higher, in a duty station within the United States on or after July 1, 1999, so long as such employee was not a U.S. citizen or permanent resident at any time within the 12 months preceding the appointment or any time thereafter.[195]

The mobility premium amount is a percentage of a the participant's salary for the employee, the spouse, and each dependent child as compensation for relocating.[196] Eligible employees hired before January 1, 2016, will receive a mobility premium or portion thereof for up to ten years.[197] Eligible employees hired on or after January 1, 2016, will receive the mobility premium for up to five years.[198]

---

190. Staff Directive 6.13. Home Country Travel.
191. *Id.* Section 3.01.
192. *Id.*
193. *Id.* Section 3.02.
194. https://www.worldbank.org/en/about/unit/human-resources/home-country-travel?cq_ck=1555697971316 (last visited May 1, 2025).
195. Staff Directive 6.21, Mobility Premium. Section 1.01.
196. *Id.* Section 1.04.
197. *Id.* Section 1.05.
198. *Id.* Section 1.06.

3.10.5.4 World Bank/IMF Couples

Where one partner is a World Bank employee and the other is an IMF employee and both are eligible for education benefits, only one may take such benefit, and that party must claim all of the children for any education benefits.[199] In the event of this couple divorcing or the IMF employee becoming ineligible for education benefits, then the World Bank employee will be eligible for education benefits, assuming all other eligibility requirements are met.[200]

Where a couple consists of two World Bank employees, if both are eligible for the mobility premium, then only one will receive it.[201] If one is eligible for the mobility premium and the other is eligible for education benefits and home travel, then the employees will have to elect which benefit they want to receive. If these couples divorce, then each will receive the benefits to which they are eligible on their own employment records.[202]

Elections made by couples to receive the education benefits/home travel in lieu of the mobility premium or vice versa are irrevocable.[203]

3.10.6 Immigration and Visas

Employees of the World Bank working in the United States must fall into one of the following immigration categories before beginning work: U.S. citizen, U.S. permanent resident, pending U.S. permanent resident with valid work permit, U.S. asylum status with valid work permit, U.S. refugee status with valid work permit, dependent "A" (diplomatic) visa with valid work permit.[204] If such person does not fall into one of these categories, then they must obtain a G4 visa.[205]

A G4 visa is a visa provided to international organization employees and their immediate family members who plan to accompany the

---

199. World Bank Staff Rule 6.14. Section 7.05.
200. *Id.* Section 7.05.
201. *Id.* Section 2.01.
202. *Id.* Section 2.02.
203. *Id.* Section 2.06.
204. G00203 Summary of Benefits Applicable to Headquarters-based Open and Term Staff, *supra* note 110.
205. *Id.*

employee on the mission.[206] If a new employee is already in the United States on a tourist or visitor visa, then they must exit the U.S. and obtain the G4 visa before beginning work.[207]

Dependent G4 visas are available for immediate family members of the new World Bank employee, to include the spouse, unmarried children under the age of 26, and parents/parents-in-law.[208] These G4 and dependent G4 visas are valid while the employee is employed by the organization and can generally be renewed within the United States so long as all information is provided timely and the employment continues.[209]

If representing the spouse, then it is important to check if they are in the United States on a visa and if so when it expires. The World Bank requires that its employees cooperate with the renewal of a dependent G4 visa, so you can reach out to the World Bank for assistance if needed.[210] If the employee is really uncooperative you may also want to consult with an immigration attorney to prevent your client from being forced out of the country in the middle of the divorce proceeding. If the employee transfers to a position outside of the United States, or leaves the employ of the World Bank, then the G4 visa status will terminate, and both parties will have to leave the U.S. unless prepared with a different means to remain within the U.S.

The World Bank reports that a G4 dependent status can be lost if the principal employee departs the United States for an overseas assignment or otherwise begins to live abroad, a final divorce decree is entered, termination of the principal employee's employment, or death of the principal employee.[211] The dependent spouse can remain

---

206. The World Bank, *Request G4/G1 Visa for the First Time,* https://www.worldbank.org/en/about/unit/human-resources/request-g1-g4-visa-for-the-first-time-outside-the-us#:~:text=G%2D4%20visas%20for%20non,or%20more%20at%20a%20time.%20 (last visited May 1, 2025).

207. *Id.*

208. *Id.*

209. *Id.*

210. *Id.*

211. *Id.* It is important to note that the World Bank reports that a physical or legal separation does not cause the spouse to lose G4 dependent status. Only a final divorce decree can do that, so the main consideration during the pendency of the divorce is whether the visa will expire before the divorce is final. *Id.*

in the United States for up to 30 days following the triggering event.[212] Once the dependent spouse leaves within those 30 days, they cannot return under the same G4 visa; the return must be under some other method of entry.[213]

Work permits for the dependent spouse also terminate upon loss of G4 dependent status, so the spouse will have to stop working as of the date of the triggering event.[214] A person can only have one immigrant visa status at a time, so in the event of a divorce and the spouse wants to remain within the United States for more than 30 days thereafter, it is important for the spouse to consult with an immigration attorney to discuss options for staying.

The World Bank takes the issue of visas seriously, and can bypass the employee in any process regarding the spouse's visa or work permit if necessary.[215] Affected persons can contact the Work Bank Group's Human Resources Visa Unit at 202-473-2222 or HROperations@worldbank.org.[216]

The family must also keep in mind the events triggering loss of the dependent child's G4 status. Those events are marriage, gaining full-time employment (if not also a full-time student), earning over $10,712 per year (unless also a full-time student), leaving the employee's household, attaining age 25 unless disabled.[217] Parties should consult an immigration attorney to discuss options for children in advance of the child losing dependent status, if possible, if they hope for the child to remain within the United States after an event triggering the loss of their status.

It is critical to consult with immigration counsel in order to protect the interests of your client.

---

212. *Id.*

213. *Id.*

214. *Id.*

215. Domestic Relations and World Bank Group Families, *supra* note 154, at Section 7.29.

216. *Id.*

217. *Id.* 5.15.

3.10.7 Request for Information Directed to the World Bank

The World Bank is immune from legal service of process as part of its privileges and immunities.[218] Therefore, no subpoena directed to the World Bank will be honored. However, the World Bank does have a provision that allows present spouses and domestic partners of past or present World Bank employees to have access to the employee's salary and benefits information (to include insurance and pension information).[219] Therefore, no matter which spouse you represent, they will have access to the financial information from the World Bank by simply submitting a written request to the HR Operations.[220] The World Bank reserves discretion as to whether or not to advise their employee if such information has been requested. As such, if there is a concern of domestic violence should the employee learn of such request, the concern should be explained to the World Bank to protect the spouse.

PRACTICE TIP

A World Bank employee* spouse *may request the following information from the World Bank directly: the employee's salary, which is their net salary, and it's estimated gross equivalent; the employee's benefits to include dependency allowance, assignment allowances, separation grant accrual termination grant restoration accrual, expatriate benefits, resettlement benefits, unused annual leave benefits, pension, insurance, and the most recent designation of benefits for the employee's pension and death benefits.

HR Operations is located at 1818 H Street, N.W., Washington, D.C. 20433 HROperations@worldbank.org, or 202-473-2222. Note the request for such information must be done in writing.

---

218. Domestic Relations and World Bank Group Families, *supra* note 154, at Section 2.7.

219. *Id.* Section 2.6.

220. *Id.*

The World Bank may provide the same information to a former spouse or former domestic partner "in connection with legal proceedings adjudicating [an employee's] personal legal obligation related to child support or alimony as evidenced by a court order."[221] Without a court order, the World Bank may provide the information based on evidence of ongoing litigation, the employee's failure to provide such information, or the existence of a minor child or minor children, only if that requested information is deemed by the World Bank to be necessary for a "fair determination of [an employee's] obligation in respect to child support or alimony" and the disclosure of such information would not cause undue hardship to the employee.[222] It is at the discretion of the World Bank if the employee will be notified of the disclosure.[223]

The address that the World Bank has on record for the employee may be shared with the spouse, former spouse, domestic partner, former domestic partner, or their legal representative.[224] However, the request made to the World Bank for such information must include a certified copy or original request from the judicial, administrative, or civil authority, spouse, former spouse, domestic partner, former domestic partner, or their legal representatives in matters of divorce, child support, and/or alimony.[225]

Similarly, service upon a World Bank Group employee cannot be accomplished on World Bank Group premises.[226] Since it is within the World Bank Group's policies that the employees will comply with local legal procedures, the World Bank Group will attempt to assist in the service of the employee.[227]

---

221. *Id.* at 73.
222. *Id.*
223. *Id.*
224. *Id.* at 74.
225. *Id.*
226. *Id.* Section 4.5.
227. *Id.* Section 4.5. Specifically, if the employee is at World Bank Group premises for work, the legal team will review the subpoena or summons to confirm that it is for the employee in their personal capacity, and then have security invite the employee off premises to accomplish service. If the employee refuses, such refusal will be noted and the employee referred for a personnel action. *Id.*

The Bank-Fund Staff Federal Credit Union, however, is a U.S. institution, and not subject to the privileges and immunities of the World Bank.[228] Therefore, the Bank-Fund Staff Federal Credit Union must comply with subpoenas, service of process, and other legal requests for information.[229]

3.10.8 Wage Garnishment for Spousal Support or Child Support

The World Bank will not honor an order to garnish an employee's wages for alimony, child support, or arrears thereof.[230] The World Bank does, however, recognize the importance of such payments and has an internal procedure to authorize such garnishment.[231] Specifically, the spouse (or attorney) should submit a copy of the court order with a cover letter explaining the entire circumstance and timeline to the World Bank Legal Department and the World Bank Group Office of Ethics and Business Conduct.[232] After receiving approval from the Legal Department, the Office of Ethics and Business Conduct will encourage the employee to comply.[233] If the employee refuses to comply within five business days, then the Office of Ethics and Business Conduct can authorize the payroll department to garnish the wages in the amount stated in the court order.[234] Regardless of the payment scheme described in the court order, the World Bank garnishments will be paid on the 15th and 30th of each applicable month.[235]

Upon being presented with a divorce decree or other court order, the World Bank will process the decree accordingly. If, however, the spouse not submitting the decree to the World Bank objects and provides proof that the decree is being challenged in court, then the World Bank will stop all actions until receiving a final order.[236]

---

228. *Id.* Section 4.7.

229. *Id.*

230. Domestic Relations and World Bank Group Families, *supra* note 154, at Section 3.4.

231. *Id.* Section 3.5.

232. *Id.* Section 3.6.

233. *Id.*

234. *Id.*

235. *Id.* Section 3.5.

236. *Id.* at 93.

Further, the World Bank will apply the preceding procedures for orders for *pendente lite* child or spousal support awards, so long as the order satisfies the World Bank requirements for a court order.[237]

3.11 Helpful Staff Rules

"Staff Rule 3.06 Family Obligations" provides ethical guidance for their employees that can be enforced through the Office of Ethics and Business Conduct (EBC).[238] The EBC is charged with ensuring the World Bank Group employees are aware of their ethical obligations, and making reports of trends, data, and lessons learned in addressing the issues.[239] The stated purpose of the Rule is so that the privileges and immunities enjoyed by the World Bank Group as an organization are not used to shield employees from their personal legal obligations or from obedience to the laws.[240]

Specifically, section 6.01(f) of Rule 3.06 states that "failure to meet personal legal obligations as required by World Bank Group policies including payment of court-ordered spousal and child support" is an act of misconduct that can be reported to the EBC. It is in an employee's best interests to comply with the internal polices, however, because they may be subject to censure, suspension from duty with or without pay (or reduced pay), demotion, reduction in pay, or separation from service for violations.[241] Rule 3.06 also applies to former employees.[242] World Bank employees cannot jeopardize their accrued pension benefits.

In the event an employee fails to cooperate, the World Bank has special disciplinary measures for matters regarding an employee's failure to cooperate in family legal obligations, specifically the payment of court-ordered spousal or child support.[243]

Section 2.02 of Rule 3.06 dictates the criteria for the World Bank to make deductions from an employee's salary for child support or

237. *Id.* at 94.
238. *Id.* Appendix A, Staff Rule 3.06 Family Obligations.
239. *Id.* Appendix A, Staff Rule 3.06.04.
240. Domestic Relations and World Bank Group Families, Appendix E, at 92.
241. *Id.* at 67.
242. *Id.* at 78.
243. *Id.* at 90.

alimony purposes.[244] The requirements are: (1) an original, certified copy or a court order that evidences an employee's legal obligation to pay a discernable amount for child support or alimony, or the employee's failure to make such payments; and (2) the employee fails to provide the EBC with proof of compliance therewith.[245] If the employee fails to provide such proof, the EBC may request additional information regarding the court order, such as proof of service on the employee.[246] The EBC will give the employee five days to get in compliance voluntarily, and if not, then the EBC will authorize a payroll deduction.[247]

In the event that the documentation provide to the World Bank does not satisfy their requirements, additional or revised documents will have to be provided.[248] Further, if the World Bank is provided with divorce decrees from two different jurisdictions, the World Bank may refuse to provide further information, and stop division of any benefits until they are presented with a decree finally adjudicating the matters.[249]

3.12 Domestic Violence Assistance

The World Bank Group has programs available for victims of domestic abuse as well as internal policies to prevent and provide consequences for those taking abusive actions. The World Bank Group has the Domestic Abuse Prevention Program (DAPP), which is a free and confidential counselling and case management program that offers services in many languages.[250] DAPP is available to World Bank employees, their spouses, and dependents.[251] DAPP can provide limited financial assistance to victims of domestic abuse to apply for a protective order.[252]

244. *Id.* at 92.
245. *Id.* at 93.
246. *Id.*
247. *Id.*
248. *Id.*
249. *Id.*
250. *Id.* at 26.
251. *Id.*
252. *Id.*

Chapter 4

United Nations

4.1 What Is the United Nations?

The United Nations is an intergovernmental organization that was created with the purpose to keep peace and security among its member nations.[1] Founded in 1945, the United Nations was formed in response to the ruins that World War II had caused to several nations.[2] The 51 founding nations spent two months drafting the UN Charter with the hope that it would prevent another world war and would provide solidarity throughout the world.[3] The United Nations officially began on October 24, 1945.[4]

The organization has grown exponentially since its formation. Now there are 193 member states.[5] Today, the United Nations employs around 37,000 people around the world, making it the largest international organization.[6] In the United States alone, there are about 6,500 United Nations employees that work at the United Nations headquarters, which is located in New York City, New York.[7] The United Nations' website is https://www.un.org/en/.

1. United Nations, *History of the United Nations*, https://www.un.org/en/about-us/history-of-the-un (last visited May 1, 2025).
2. *Id.*
3. *Id.*
4. *Id.*
5. *Id.*
6. United Nations, *#Work4UN: Basic Facts About Working for the United Nations*, https://www.un.org/en/academic-impact/work4un-basic-facts-about-working-united-nations (last visited May 1, 2025).
7. *Id.*

4.2 Overview of United Nations Joint Staff Pension Fund (UNJSPF)

4.2.1 How It Works/Funding

The United Nations Joint Staff Pension Fund (UNJSPF) is currently valued at approximately $82 billion as of March 2023. Weekly and monthly investment figures are available on the pension fund website www.unjspf.org. UNJSPF had 219,573 participants and beneficiaries as of December 31, 2021.

The UNJSPF was established in 1949 by the General Assembly through Resolution 248 (III) to provide retirement, death, disability, and related benefits for staff of the United Nations and the other organizations admitted to membership in the UNJSPF. As an independent inter-agency entity, the UNJSPF operates under its own regulations as approved by the General Assembly and, in accordance with its governance structure, is administered by the United Nations Joint Staff Pension Board, which currently consists of 33 members, representing the 25 member organizations. The UNJSPF has offices in New York and Switzerland, and two liaison offices in Nairobi, Kenya, and Bangkok, Thailand.[8]

Member organizations of the UNJSPF are specialized agencies that have a relationship with the United Nations.[9] Certain organizations are recommended to the Pension Fund, and then the General Assembly must determine which organizations are admitted.[10] The following specialized agencies are current member organizations:[11]

1. Preparatory Commission for the Comprehensive Nuclear-Test-Ban Treaty Organization (CTBTO)
2. European and Mediterranean Plant Protection Organization (EPPO)
3. Food and Agriculture Organization of the United Nations (FAO)
4. International Atomic Energy Agency (IAEA)

8. https://www.unjspf.org/about-us/about-the-fund/.
9. *Id.*
10. *Id.*
11. https://www.unjspf.org/about-us/member-organizations/.

5. International Centre for Genetic Engineering and Biotechnology (ICGEB)
6. International Centre for the Study of the Preservation and the Restoration of Cultural Property (ICCROM)
7. International Civil Aviation Organization (ICAO)
8. International Criminal Court (ICC)
9. International Fund for Agricultural Development (IFAD)
10. International Labour Organization (ILO)
11. International Maritime Organization (IMO)
12. International Organization for Migration (IOM)
13. Inter Parliamentary Union (IPU)
14. International Seabed Authority (ISA)
15. International Telecommunication Union (ITU)
16. International Tribunal for the Law of the Sea (ITLOS)
17. Special Tribunal for Lebanon (STL)
18. United Nations (UN)
19. United Nations Educational Scientific and Cultural Organization (UNESCO)
20. United Nations Industrial Development Organization (UNIDO)
21. Wassenaar Arrangement on Export Controls for Conventional Arms and Dual-Use Goods & Technologies (WA)
22. World Health Organization (WHO)
23. World Intellectual Property Organization (WIPO)
24. World Meteorological Organization (WMO)
25. World Tourism Organization (UNWTO)

Both participants and the employer (member organization) make contributions to the UNJSPF concurrently as the participant accrues contributory service.[12] Contributions are made at the following rates, based on the participant's pensionable remuneration[13] at the time of service:[14]

---

12. Regulations, Rules, and Pension Adjustment System of the United Nations Joint Staff Pension Fund, Article 25 (Jan. 1, 2022).

13. *See* Terminology, Section 4.4 herein.

14. Regulations, *supra* note 12.

Contributory Service Accrued	Participant Contribution	Employing Member Organization Contribution
Before 1984	7.00%	14.00%
January 1, 1984, through Juned 30, 1988	7.25%	14.50%
July 1, 1988, through June 30, 1989	7.40%	14.80%
July 1, 1989, through December 31, 1989	7.50%	15.00%
After January 1, 1990	7.90%	15.90%

In the event a participant is on leave without pay, they shall continue to make their contribution, as shall the employing member organization, and shall continue to accrue contributory service during such period of leave without pay for so long as the contributions are made.[15]

The UNJSPF provides annual statements to their employees which outline the amount of contributions made by the participant, the date the participant joined, and provides estimates of the pension payments.[16]

PRACTICE TIP

Participants are able to run pension estimates at any time through the online portal.

4.2.2 Who Is Eligible to Participate

Any full-time employee of the United Nations (or a member organization) who is appointed to a position whose term is six months or longer or an employee who completes six months of full-time

15. *Id.* The participant and the employing member organization may share responsibility of making the contributions in any manner they deem appropriate. *Id.*

16. UNJSPF Handout from the April 6, 2023, UNJSPF Global Town hall.

employment within the United Nations (or a member organization) is a participant in the UNJSPF.[17] Employees remain participants in the UNJSPF until they terminate employment with the United Nations (or member organizations), die, or the employing organization is no longer a member organization.[18] However, such participation will be deemed not to have ceased if the employee again becomes a participant within 36 months and did not receive a benefit from the UNJSPF.[19]

4.2.3 Eligibility for Retirement

A participant is eligible for an immediate pension benefit if they have reached their normal retirement age and have at least five years of contributory service.[20] A participant's normal retirement age is based on their initial hire date with the UN. More details can be found in Section 4.4, Terminology, herein.

Pension benefits with respect to contributory service periods commencing on or after January 1, 1983, are calculated by multiplying the participant's final average remuneration by a specified percentage for specified periods of service, as described herein:[21]

Years of Service	Percent Multiplier
1–5	1.50%
6–10	1.75%
11–35	2.00%
36+ (performed after July 1, 1995)	1.00%

In this chart, a period of contributory service of five years or longer and ending between January 1, 1978, and December 31, 1982, shall be included in the first 35 years of service at the rates listed therein.[22]

17. Regulations, *supra* note 12, at Article 21.
18. *Id.*
19. *Id.*
20. *Id.* Article 28.
21. *Id.* The pension benefit is capped at a maximum of 70 percent of the participant's final average remuneration.
22. *Id.*

Periods of contributory service commencing before January 1, 1983, result in a calculation of a retirement benefit as follows:[23]

Years of Service	Percent Multiplier
1–30	2.0%
31–35	1.0%
35+ (performed after July 1, 1995)	1.0%

There is a cap on the pension benefit of 70 percent of the participant's final average remuneration.[24]

4.2.3.1 *Early Retirement*

Employees beginning their participation in the plan before January 1, 2014. Such employees are eligible for an early retirement benefit if they separate from service after attaining age 55 but before their normal retirement age if they also have at least five years of contributory service in the plan.[25] The benefit amount shall be calculated as the standard benefit, but reduced at the rate of 6 percent for each year that the participant was younger than their normal retirement age as of the date they separated from service.[26] However, if the participant served between 25 and 30 years, then their benefit shall only be reduced by 2 percent per year for service performed before January 1, 1985, and reduced by 3 percent per year for service performed after January 1, 1985.[27] Additionally, if a participant's service is 30 years or more, then their benefit shall be reduced only by 1 percent per year. These reduction rates shall apply for up to five years.[28]

Employees beginning their participation in the plan on or after January 1, 2014. Such employees are eligible for an early retirement if they separate from service at age 58 but before their normal retirement age of 65 years old if they have at least five years of contributory

23. *Id.*
24. *Id.*
25. *Id.* Article 29(a).
26. *Id.* Article 29(b).
27. *Id.*
28. *Id.*

service in the plan.[29] The benefit amount shall be calculated as their standard benefit, but reduced at the rate of 6 percent per year that the participant was younger than age 65 on the date they separated service.[30] However, if a participant has at least 25 years of contributory service, then their benefit shall be reduced by 4 percent per year.[31] Such smaller reduction rate would apply for up to five years.[32]

4.2.3.2 Deferred Retirement Benefit

A participant who separates from service prior to their normal retirement age with at least five years of service can wait until their normal retirement age or their early retirement age to commence the receipt benefits from the plan.[33] The benefit shall be calculated at the rate for normal or early retirement, as is appropriate for the participant's retirement benefits commencement date.[34]

4.2.3.3 Eligibility for Benefits and Reentry as a Participant

If a participant terminates their service and is eligible for a benefit under the plan, such eligibility to commence benefits will be suspended if the participant is later reemployed by the UN and is an active participant in the plan.[35] The participant will be eligible for their original benefits when they later terminate service and participation in the plan.[36] In addition, the participant will be eligible for benefits from their second period of participation in the plan either on that period's own eligibility, or the participant can merge the two periods of employment.[37] In the event a participant is reemployed, their benefit is capped at the amount they would have received had their employment been continuous.[38]

---

29. *Id.* Article 29(c).
30. *Id.*
31. *Id.*
32. *Id.*
33. *Id.* Article 30(a).
34. *Id.* Article 30(b).
35. *Id.* Article 40.
36. *Id.*
37. *Id.* Note, this is markedly different than the IDB's procedures here which prohibit the merging of employment periods to determine the pension benefit. See Section 2.1.4.
38. *Id.*

4.2.3.4 *Timing of Benefit Selection*

A participant may delay their selection of a deferred retirement benefit or a withdrawal benefit for up to 36 months after the date of their separation.[39] If a participant does not make a decision within the 36-month election deferral period and they are younger than their normal retirement age on the date of the separation from service, then they shall be deemed to have elected a deferred retirement benefit.[40]

4.3 Disability Benefit

A disability is benefit is payable to a participant who is determined by the board to be incapacitated for service in a position that is reasonably compatible with their skills in a member organization due to an illness or injury that is likely to be permanent or of a long duration.[41] Such disability benefit shall continue for the duration of the illness or injury following separation from the UN or the expiration of paid leave, so long as by the time the participant reaches seven years younger than their normal retirement age the illness or injury is deemed to be permanent.[42]

The disability benefit shall be calculated as the amount of the participant's normal retirement benefit if the participant is at least their normal retirement age.[43] If the participant is younger than their normal retirement age, then their benefit shall be calculated as if they had continued to work until their normal retirement age and maintained their final average remuneration.[44]

The disability benefit can be converted to a withdrawal benefit or a deferred retirement benefit if it is discontinued due to the termination of the illness or injury.[45] In such an event, the benefit would be calculated as of the date of commencement for the disability benefit.[46]

---

39. *Id.* Article 32.
40. *Id.*
41. *Id.* Article 33.
42. *Id.* In cases where the participant's normal retirement age is 60 years old, they will have to be at least 55 years old and the illness or injury will be deemed to be permanent.
43. *Id.*
44. *Id.*
45. *Id.*
46. *Id.*

In addition, the disability benefit can be suspended if the participant is otherwise in paid employment with a member organization.[47] Further, the benefit can be reduced if the participant is otherwise engaged in paid employment, despite the illness or injury continuing.[48]

4.4 Terminology

The UNJSPF glossary defines key terms used by the fund. Most of these terms are defined by the fund's regulations and rules, but according to the UNJSPF website, some words have "taken a life of their own after being used for 70 years by the Fund."[49]

Administrative Rules.[50] The rules made by the board under Article 4.

Beneficiaries.[51] Those entitled to a disability benefit, as well as those who are entitled to regular, periodic survivor's benefit from the fund (e.g., entitled to surviving spouse(s)/ex-spouse(s)/child(ren)/secondary dependent).

Benefit.[52] A payment made from the fund to include a withdrawal settlement under Article 31, and a residual settlement under Article 38.

Contributory Service.[53] Service accrued by a participant in the UNJSPF from the date of hire through the date they terminate participation.

Divorced Surviving Spouse.[54] The former spouse of a participant or retiree who requests a divorced spouse's benefit and meets the retirement set forth in Article 35bis(b) of the UNJSPF regulations.

Equivalent Actuarial Value.[55] The equivalent value determined according to the actuarial tables adopted by the board under Article 11.

---

47. *Id.*
48. *Id.*
49. https://web.archive.org/web/20230723185826/https://www.unjspf.org/resources/glossary/.
50. Regulations, *supra* note 12, at Article 22.
51. *Id.*
52. *Id.*
53. *Id.*
54. *Id.*
55. *Id.*

Final Average Remuneration.[56] The average annual pensionable remuneration of a participant during:

1. The 36 completed calendar months of highest pensionable remuneration within the last five years of a participant's contributory service; or
2. If the contributory service was less than five years, the 36 completed calendar months of highest pensionable remuneration within the actual period of such service; or
3. If the contributory service contained less than 36 completed calendar months, the actual number of such months within the contributory service; or
4. If the contributory service contained no completed calendar month, the actual period of such service.

Fund.[57] United Nations Joint Staff Pension Fund also referred to as "the fund."

Normal Retirement Age.[58] Participants beginning service with the UNJSPF on or after January 1, 2014, have a normal retirement age of 65 years; participants beginning service between January 1, 1990, through December 31, 2013, have a normal retirement age of 62 years; and any participant beginning service on or before December 31, 1989, have a normal retirement age of 60 years.[59]

Pensionable Remuneration.[60] The employee's gross pensionable salary plus subsequent additions thereto, plus language allowances, plus a nonresident's allowance, if applicable, at its equivalent in dollars.

Restoration.[61] The inclusion in contributory service of the prior contributory service of a former participant who again becomes a participant.

---

56. *Regulations, Rules and Pension Adjustment System of the United Nations Joint Staff Pension Fund*, Article I at 1 (Jan. 1, 2024), https://www.unjspf.org/wp-content/uploads/2024/01/2024-UNJSPF-Regulations-1-January-2024-English-1.pdf.
57. *Id.* Article I at 2.
58. *Id.* Article I.
59. *Id.*
60. *Id.*
61. *Id.*

Separation.[62] Ceasing to be in the service of a member organization by means other than death.

The Board.[63] Board means the United Nations Joint Staff Pension Board. The Pension Board is a subsidiary of the UN General Assembly. The board administers the fund and it protects the best interest of the UNJSPF participants and beneficiaries by setting strategic goals and policies, providing general oversight and monitoring.

Validation.[64] The inclusion in contributory service of a period of noncontributory service that occurred prior to the commencement of participation.[65]

4.5 Commutation of Benefits

A participant may commute up to one-third of the actuarial equivalent of the pension benefit at or before the time the participant begins to receive pension benefits.[66] However, if such amount is less than the amount of contributions the participant made during their employment, then the amount of commuted benefits shall equal the amount of the participant's contributions.[67] If the actuarial equivalent of the participant's benefit is less than $1,000, up to the full actuarial value of the benefit, including the prospective spouse's benefit (if the participant is married), may be commuted.[68]

PRACTICE TIP

The plan participant may commute up to one-third of their benefit prior to going into pay status. A marital settlement, court, or spouse cannot limit their ability to make this election.

62. *Id.*
63. *Id.* Article 5.
64. *Id.* Article 23.
65. *Glossary,* UNJSPF, https://www.unjspf.org/resources/glossary/ (2024), *supra* note 49.
66. https://www.unjspf.org/about-us/about-the-fund/, Article 28.
67. *Id.* Article 28(g)(ii).
68. *Id.* Article 28.

A commutation of benefits on an early retirement benefit is calculated based on the actuarial equivalent of the participant's normal retirement benefit had the participant retired on their normal retirement date with the same number of years of service and final remuneration.[69] Stated differently, only the monthly payments are reduced for an early retirement or any commuted benefit elected.

A participant with a deferred retirement benefit can only commute their benefit if the actuarial equivalent is $1,000 or less, in which case the full amount of the benefit shall be paid as a commuted benefit.[70]

4.6 Withdrawal Benefit

A withdrawal benefit shall be payable to the participant if they separate from service and do not qualify for a normal, early, or deferred retirement benefit.[71] An example of such a scenario is if the participant does not have at least five years of contributory service on the date of separation. The benefit is calculated as the participant's contributions to the plan if the participant had less than five years of contributory service.[72]

If the participant had over five years of contributory service they may elect to receive a withdrawal benefit and terminate their interest in the UNJSPF. If they elect to receive a withdrawal benefit, then it is calculated as their contributions to the plan, increased by 10 percent per year in excess of five years of service, up to a maximum of a 100 percent increase in their contributions.[73]

A participant who returns to the employ of the UN may elect to repay any withdrawal benefit received to restore their prior pension entitlement.[74] If the participant elects to restore such service period, they must return to the fund the full withdrawal benefit or other funds received at their termination of service, plus interest thereon.[75] Such

69. *Id.* Article 28(g)(i)(B).
70. *Id.* Article 30(c).
71. *Id.* Article 31.
72. *Id.*
73. *Id.*
74. *Id.* Article 24. *See also* Section 4.6 herein regarding the Withdrawal Benefit.
75. *Id.*

election must be made within one year of recommencing employment with the United Nations or a member organization.[76] If such election is made, the participant's commencement start date is the date applicable to the period of service that was restored.[77] If there is a break in periods of service, then at retirement the service periods will be aggregated to determine the total contributory service.[78]

A participant may also increase their pension benefit by electing to validate prior service that was not eligible for participation in the UNJSPF previously.[79] To do this, the participant would have to make a lump sum payment of the contributions that would have been made to the UNJSPF had the service been eligible. If such payment is made with marital funds, but the time of the service completed was prior to the marriage, then the parties must determine how the time will be treated and describe it correctly in any agreement.

PRACTICE TIP

If an employee leaves the UN, they may take a withdrawal benefit as a lump sum and void their participation in the pension. The withdrawal benefit is calculated as their contributions to the plan, increased by 10 percent per year (in excess of five years of service), up to a maximum of a 100 percent increase in their contributions.

4.7 Death and Survivor Benefits

4.7.1 Widow(er)'s Benefit

A widow's benefit is available to a female spouse of a participant who was entitled to a retirement benefit.[80] Similarly, a widower's benefit is available to a male spouse of a participant who was entitled to a

76. *Id.*
77. *Id.*
78. *Id.* Article 22.
79. *Id.* Article 23.
80. *Id.* Article 34.

retirement benefit.[81] The benefits available to a widow or widower are the same.[82]

Although the language in the regulations does use the terms "female" and "male" with respect to surviving spouses, it seems to be a holdover from the traditional definition of "widow" and "widower" and not intended as a limitation based on the recipient's gender identity. In fact, the UNJSPF has forms available for continuation of health insurance coverage and designation of beneficiaries both of which include "other" as a gender category.

A widow(er)'s benefit is not payable if the participant dies during a period of leave without pay unless the widow(er) would have been eligible for such benefit had the participant died on the day before beginning their period of leave without pay.[83]

The widow(er)'s benefit is payable on regular increments for the life of the widow(er).[84] If, however, the annual benefit is $600 or less, then the benefit shall be payable in a lump sum.[85] The benefit payable to the widow(er) is one-half the full benefit payable to the participant/retiree.[86]

4.7.2 Death in Service or Prior to Receiving Retirement Benefits

To be eligible for a widow(er)'s benefit the spouse must have been married to the participant on the date of death, if the participant's death occurred during employment.[87] The annual amount of such benefit shall be one-half of the annual amount of the retirement benefit the participant would have been eligible for on the date of death, or one-half the actual entitlement if the participant was already entitled

---

81. *Id.* Article 35.
82. *Id.*
83. *Id.* Article 39.
84. *Id.* Article 34(f).
85. *Id.*
86. United Nations Joint Staff Pension Fund. Divorce Handbook (May 2010).
87. *Regulations, Rules and Pension Adjustment System of the United Nations Joint Staff Pension Fund, supra* note 56, at Article 34(a).

to a benefit.[88] However, the widow(er)'s benefit shall not be smaller than $750 per year.[89]

4.7.3 Death After Terminating Service

To be eligible for a widow(er)'s benefit the spouse must have been married to the participant on the date of termination of service and stayed married to the participant until the date of death.[90] The annual amount of the benefit shall be one-half of the annual amount the participant was entitled to as of the date of death.[91] The same minimums apply as for a participant who dies while in service.[92] If the participant had commuted any part of their benefit then the widow(er)'s benefit is calculated as if no commutation were made.[93]

If the participant dies after beginning to receive retirement benefits, the widow(er)'s benefit is half the amount of the participant's benefit.[94] Similarly, the benefit is calculated based on the amount of the participant's benefit without having commuted any benefit.[95]

In the event that there are multiple surviving spouses (in cases of plural marriage),[96] this benefit is divided equally among them.[97] When a surviving spouse dies, their benefit is distributed among the remaining surviving spouses.[98]

---

88. *Id.* Article 34.
89. *Id.* Article 34(c)(ii).
90. *Id.* Article 34(a).
91. *Id.* Article 34.
92. *Id.* Article 34(c).
93. *Id.* Article 34(b).
94. *Id.* Article 34(e).
95. *Id.*
96. A surviving spouse is a person married to the participant on their last day of service and at the time pension benefits commence. In order for multiple of such persons to exist, the participant must be in a polygamous relationship. *See* Section 4.8 herein.
97. *Regulations, Rules and Pension Adjustment System of the United Nations Joint Staff Pension Fund, supra* note 56, at Article 34(g).
98. *Id.*

4.7.4 Divorced Surviving Spouse Benefit

The former spouse of a participant or former participant may request a benefit directly from the plan so long as the following conditions are met: [99]

1. Participant and the former spouse were married for a period of at least ten years during which the participant contributed to the fund;
2. The participant's death was within 15 years of the date of divorce, unless at the time of death the participant was under a legal obligation to provide support for the former spouse;
3. The former spouse is at least 40 years old, or, if younger than 40 years old, the benefit is not payable until the former spouse reaches 40 years of age; and
4. The former spouse must not have waived interest in the UNJSPF benefits in the separate agreement or divorce document.

The amount of the divorced surviving spouse benefit is one-half the retiree's full pension benefit, if no widow(er)'s benefit is payable and the retiree separated from service on or after April 1, 1999.[100] If there are multiple divorced surviving spouses and/or widow(er)s, then the benefit shall be divided between all surviving spouses in proportion to the length of marriage to the participant.[101] If the retiree separated from service before April 1, 1999, then the divorced surviving spouse's benefit is a fixed amount of approximately $9,337 per year.[102]

PRACTICE TIP

The UN plan allows multiple (divorced) surviving spouses to be survivors of the pension.

99. *Id.* Article 35 *bis*.
100. *Id.* Article 35 *bis* (c).
101. *Id.*
102. DIVORCE HANDBOOK, *supra* note 86.

4.7.5 Marriage After Beginning UNJSPF Benefits

If a participant wishes to provide a survivor benefit for a spouse who the participant married *after* beginning benefits in the UNJSPF, the participant must file an election.[103] The election must be made within 12 months of the date of marriage and will become effective 18 months after the date of marriage.[104] Once the election is effective, the participant's benefit will be actuarily reduced to provide the survivor benefit for the new spouse.[105] Such election is only revokable until the death of said spouse, or divorce therefrom. Proof of death and a request to revoke the election must be provided to the plan administrator.[106] Any payments received by the plan via the actuarial reduction from the participant's benefit will not be returned to the participant upon the revocation of the election.[107]

This benefit is subject to a few restrictions. Specifically, the benefit cannot be larger than the benefit payable to the participant after the actuarial reduction to provide the benefit is applied.[108] Also, the benefit's actuarial reduction cannot cause the benefit payable to the participant to be less than one-half of the unreduced benefit.[109]

4.7.6 Child Benefit

Children are eligible recipients of the child benefit from the UNJSPF if they are the child of a participant who was eligible for benefits from the plan and who died while in service and the child was under the age of 21 at the time of the participant's death.[110] Benefit payments to the child will terminate when the child turn age 21.[111] A child who is over the age of 21 can continue to receive benefit payments if the child is "incapacitated by illness or injury for substantial gainful employment"

103. *Id.* Article 35*ter.*
104. *Id.*
105. *Id.*
106. *Id.*
107. *Id.*
108. *Id.*
109. *Id.*.
110. *Id.* Article 36.
111. *Id.*

and was receiving benefit payments before age 21, and such payments shall continue for as long as the incapacity.[112]

The amount of the child's benefit shall be one-third of the amount of a disability benefit that would have been paid to the participant had the participant retired on disability on their date of death.[113] The benefit is subject to a minimum of $300 annually.[114] The benefit may be increased if there is no surviving parent to support the child, but the maximum benefit payable is $1,800 per year.[115]

Such benefit is not payable if the participant dies during a period of leave without pay unless the child would have been eligible for such benefit had the participant died on the day before beginning their period of leave without pay.[116]

Note, this benefit is not divisible in any divorce proceeding or by court order, but this information is provided for information purposes to describe the full scope of benefits available from the plan.

4.7.7 Secondary Dependent's Benefit

The participant may have other people that they financially support, such as siblings or parents. This benefit may be available for those persons in the event of the participant's death if the participant was entitled to benefit from the plan on the date of death. Such benefit is only available to one beneficiary and is not payable if there is a benefit payable to a child, surviving spouse, or divorced surviving spouse. Further, in the case where the dependent is a sibling, the benefit is not payable if the benefit available to the participant was a deferred retirement benefit.[117] Finally, such benefit is also not payable if the participant dies during a period of leave without pay unless the dependent would have been eligible for such benefit had the participant died on the day before beginning their period of leave without pay.[118]

---

112. *Id.*
113. *Id.* Article 36(d).
114. *Id.*
115. *Id.* Article 36 (e) & (f).
116. *Id.* Article 39.
117. *Id.* Article 37.
118. *Id.* Article 39.

The benefit amount payable to a sibling shall be paid at the child benefit rate.[119] The benefit amount payable to a parent shall be paid at the widow(er)'s benefit rate.[120] If more than one person is eligible for such benefit, then the board will select the beneficiary of the benefit.[121]

Note, this benefit is not divisible in any divorce proceeding or by court order, but this information is provided for information purposes to describe the full scope of benefits available from the plan.

4.7.8 Residual Benefit

In the event that all benefits described herein from the plan have been paid and they do not equal the amount of contributions the participant had paid, there is a residual benefit payment available to the participant's designated beneficiary.[122] If there is no living beneficiary at the time this benefit is to be paid, then the payment shall be made to the participant's estate.[123]

As this benefit is only available if there are contributions remaining after all other benefits are paid, it is unlikely that any benefit payable as the residual would be substantial. However, since this payment is made to the participant's designated beneficiary, the parties may negotiate for the former spouse to be listed as the beneficiary of this benefit in addition to any divorce spouse survivor benefit.

A word of caution in negotiations: if this benefit is to exist in a case, it is likely to be a small benefit. Therefore the amount of time spent negotiating for it may quickly outweigh the benefit received. If the parties do agree for the former spouse to be the designated beneficiary, then it is important to have the beneficiary form executed and submitted *after* the date of divorce. Many beneficiary designation forms automatically terminate upon divorce. So the best way to secure the benefit for the former spouse is to have the participant execute the form the day after the divorce and immediately submit it

119. *Id.* Article 37.
120. *Id.*
121. *Id.*
122. *Id.* Article 38.
123. *Id.*

to the plan with a copy of the separation agreement or divorce document stating the parties' desire for the former spouse to receive such benefit.

4.8 Polygamous Relationships

Polygamy, often religiously rooted, is the practice of being married to multiple spouses concurrently.[124] Polygyny, where one husband has multiple wives, is the most common form of polygamy in the United States and throughout the rest of the world.[125] Polygamy has been illegal in the United States since 1882.

Worldwide, polygyny is legal in 58 out of almost 200 sovereign states.[126] Most of the 58 sovereign states allowing polygyny are Muslim-prominent countries located in Africa and Asia.[127] This may seem like a strikingly large statistic, but in reality, only about 2 percent of the global population lives and remains in polygamous households.[128]

Polygamy can be most densely found in the sub-Saharan African region of the world. Approximately 11 percent of such population lives in a polygamous arrangement.[129] Additionally, in "the 'polygamy belt,' [of western Africa] stretching from Senegal to Tanzania, it is common for more than one third of married women to be polygamous."[130]

In contrast to parts of Africa and Asia, polygamy is illegal throughout the entire European Union.[131] Yet, polygamy is often indi-

---

124. Legal Information Institute, *Polygamy,* https://www.law.cornell.edu/wex/polygamy #:~:text=Polygamy%20is%20the%20practice%20of,In%20Murphy%20v (last visited May 1, 2025).

125. Thomas Brooks, *The Problem with Polygamy,* 37 Global Gender Just. 109 (2009).

126. *Legality of Polygamy,* Encyclopedia.Pub (Dec. 6, 2022), https://encyclopedia.pub/entry/37734.

127. *Id.*

128. Stephanie Kramer, *Polygamy Is Rare Around the World and Mostly Confined to a Few Regions,* Pew Rsch. Ctr. (Dec. 7, 2020), https://www.pewresearch.org/short-reads/2020/12/07/polygamy-is-rare-around-the-world-and-mostly-confined-to-a-few-regions/.

129. *Id.*

130. James Fenske, *African Polygamy: Past and Present,* 117 J. Dev. Econ. 58 (2015).

131. Polygamy in the European Union, 2005 O.J. (C327).

rectly supported in certain European countries.[132] France sets a strong example for the indirect acceptance of polygamy—where the marital status of a foreign individual is highly respected and immigrants can send for multiple wives in order to be reunited.[133] This is a stark contrast to the position of the United States. Although it is unlikely to come across a family with multiple spouses in the United States, due to its commonality in Africa and Asia and the international nature of the United Nations, it is possible to have such a family as clients and thus it is worthwhile to be aware of the restrictions on benefits. For example, for both United Nations and World Bank employees, the health insurance programs provided for staff recognize only one spouse as an eligible dependent on the plan.[134] That means that for international staff members in polygamous marriages, not all of their spouses can be covered under the health insurance provided by the organization.

4.9 Cost of Living Adjustments

Cost of living adjustments are made to the pension and survivor benefit in April of each year. A history of Consumer Price Index adjustments is available on the UNJSPF website: https://www.unjspf.org/resources/exchange-rate-tables/.

4.10 Transfers to Other Institutions

The UNJSPF has agreements with many other international organizations for the transfer of pension benefits in the event of a change in employment between these organizations. The organizations are as follows:

1. African Development Bank
2. Asian Development Bank

---

132. *Id.*

133. *Id.*

134. United Nations Health & Life Insurance Section, *FAQs*, https://www.un.org/insurance/content/faqs-0#:~:text=What%20are%20eligible%20dependants%3F,%2C%20oneUNOPS%2C%20etc.); The World Bank, *Human Resources*, https://www.worldbank.org/en/about/unit/human-resources/Enroll-or-add-dependent-on-amip-for-active-staff.

3. Council of Europe
4. European Centre for Medium-Range Weather Forecasts
5. European Space Agency
6. European Union Institution for Security Studies
7. European Organization for the Exploitation of Meteorological Satellites
8. European Investment Bank
9. European Investment Fund
10. European Bank for Reconstruction and Development
11. European Communities
12. European Free Trade Association
13. European Organization for the Safety of Air Navigation
14. Government of Canada
15. Inter-American Development Bank
16. International Monetary Fund
17. North Atlantic Treaty Organization
18. Organization for Economic Cooperation and Development
19. Organisation for the Prohibition of Chemical Weapons
20. European Union Satellite Centre
21. Provident Scheme of the Universal Postal Union
22. World Trade Organization
23. World Bank Group

The UNJSPF has an agreement with each organization listed to describe whether the transfer of pension interests is recognized as dollar for dollar, or if there is a calculation necessary to convert employment time or remuneration from one organization to another. See Section 1.4.2.1 for a description of the agreement with the IMF and Section 3.4.1 for a description of the agreement with the World Bank Group.

4.11 Division in Divorce

4.11.1 How to Divide the Employee Pension

The parties must submit a court order (not called a QDRO) to the UNJSPF that clearly describes the amount as a percent or flat dollar amount.[135] Many states have a form of coverture fraction used

135. UNJSPF Article 45.

to describe a pension award to a former spouse. The UNJSPF will not accept a court order that describes the former spouse's share via coverture fraction. It must be a clear percent or dollar amount per month.

PRACTICE TIP

The UNJSPF will not accept an order that describes a former spouse's benefit via coverture fraction. It must be a defined dollar amount or percent.

The payment will continue until the first to occur of death of the participant or death of the former spouse and is generally irrevocable.[136] However, the UNJSPF will accept a request of either party to discontinue or alter the payment amount if based on a court order or settlement agreement incorporated into a court order.[137] Any settlement agreement describing terms of the division of the participant's UNJSPF interest must also be submitted to the UNJSPF.

As such, the way to ensure that the proper amount of the pension is being paid to the former spouse is to prepare two orders. The first would be submitted at the time of divorce and include a payment amount to set a minimum payment to the former spouse. The settlement agreement would also specify that the parties intend to recalculate the former spouse's percent within a certain amount of time of the participant commencing the pension benefit, and that the parties will cooperate to reconcile any payments made by the UNJSPF before the second order is implemented.

4.11.2 How to Divide the Divorced Surviving Spouse Benefit

The divorced surviving spouse benefit is a creature of the UNJSPF. The amount available to the former spouse is one-half the amount of the unreduced benefit payable to the participant, if there is no widow(er) benefit payable. If there is a widow(er) benefit payable, or another former spouse that satisfies the requirements to receive the

136. *Id.*
137. *Id.*

divorce surviving spouse benefit then the UNJSPF reserves the right to divide the benefit among the surviving spouses in proportion to the length of their respective marriages to the participant.[138]

The former spouse can, however, waive all or a portion of their interest in the employee-spouse's UNJSPF interest. Such waiver must be clear.

4.11.3 How to Allocate Cost of Survivor Benefit

The UNJSPF will not accept an order that purports to shift the reduction for a survivor benefit for a former spouse. The parties will have to take this reduction into account when preparing their order if they wish for it to be shifted, by adjusting the dollar or percent award to the former spouse.

4.11.4 Treatment of Post-Divorce Salary Adjustments

The UNJSPF will not accept an order that purports to divide anything other than the final pension valuation. As such, if the parties wish to limit the former spouse's benefit to the amount earned as of a prior date, the participant should log into their member benefit account online and prepare an estimate as of the desired date. The parties can then reduce the former spouse's share to a dollar amount that can be inserted into the order dividing the pension.

4.11.5 Contact Information

Postal Mailing Address

United Nations Joint Staff Pension Fund
c/o United Nations
P.O. Box 5036
New York, NY 10163-5036
Courier and Registered Mailing Address
United Nations Joint Staff Pension Fund
885 Second Avenue, 37th floor, 1 DHP
New York, NY 10017
(212) 963-6931
(212) 963-3146 (fax)

138. UNJSPF FAQ, https://www.unjspf.org/for-clients/survivors-benefit/.

4.12 Remarriage of Either Party

The payments from the UNJSPF are intended to continue until the first of the parties die. As such, the remarriage of either party does not impact the payment of the pension to the former spouse during the participant's lifetime.

The survivor benefit, however, may be decreased if there are multiple surviving spouses such that the surviving spouses receive a share of the benefit relative to the length of their marriage to the participant.

4.13 Other Benefits

4.13.1 Health Benefits

All staff members of the United Nations are required to enroll and contribute to the medical insurance plan (MIP).[139] Their eligible family members (to include one spouse and eligible children) may participate but are not required.[140] The spouse must be recognized by the UN as a spouse. An eligible child must be the participant's dependent, and is eligible only until the end of the year in which they reach 25 years old, or they marry or are employed full time.[141]

Former staff members are eligible to participate in after-service health insurance if they desire.[142] The spouse and dependent children already enrolled on the participant's MIP on the date the participant separates from service as well as any child born to the participant within 300 days of separation are eligible to be covered on the participant's after-service health insurance plan.[143]

4.13.2 Life Insurance

Participation in the group life insurance program is completely voluntary.[144] The program is available to all UN staff members with an appointment of at least six months or longer, and have provided

139. MIP Presentation, April 16, 2024.
140. *Id.*
141. *Id.*
142. *Id.*
143. *Id.*
144. https://www.un.org/insurance/content/life-insurance (Apr. 30, 2024).

medical clearance. Costs will vary based on coverage levels elected. Policies may be assigned or, alternatively, the employee may make an irrevocable designation of beneficiary.

4.13.3 College Tuition and Expenses

Staff members may be eligible for an education grant.[145] To be eligible for the grant, the member must be an international recruit holding a fixed-term, continuing or permanent appointment, serving outside their home country and having a child in full-time attendance at an educational institution at a primary level or above.[146]

The staff member may also be eligible to receive boarding assistance if the child attends school outside the duty country, or in special circumstances within the duty country but outside of a reasonable commuting distance.[147]

The following fees are eligible for payment by the UN through the education grant:

> (a) Mandatory enrolment-related fees, which are required for the enrolment of a child in an educational institution. Such fees include but are not limited to admission, application, registration, enrolment, matriculation, orientation and assessment or examination fees;
>
> (b) Tuition for full-time attendance that is paid directly to the educational institution and certified by the educational institution as being necessary for attendance;
>
> (c) Tuition in the native language of the staff member if all of the conditions below are met:
>
> > (i) Instruction is given by a qualified teacher certified in the language of instruction who is not a member of the staff member's family;
> >
> > (ii) The staff member serves in a country whose language is different from the staff member's mother tongue;

---

145. Administrative Instruction: Education grant and related benefits. ST/AI/2018/1.
146. *Id.*
147. *Id.*

(iii) The child attends a local educational institution in which the instruction is given in a different language from the staff member's mother tongue;

If both parents are United Nations staff members, tuition can be in either or all of the mother tongues as defined by the staff members upon initial appointment or based on their recognized nationality in the case of multiple mother tongues;

(d) Expenses for distance learning, including blended learning, when prior written approval is obtained and such courses meet one of the following conditions:

(i) They are the only available substitute for full-time attendance at an educational institution of a type not available at the duty station;

(ii) They are related to academic subjects that are not included in the regular curriculum but are required for the child's subsequent education;

(e) Following certification by the school, expenses for private tuition provided by a teacher who is qualified in the subject concerned and is not a member of the staff member's family when one of the following conditions is met:

(i) A child attends a local educational institution, and tuition in the language of the duty station is a precondition for admittance;

(ii) A supplement to correspondence courses for which expenses are admissible under section 3.1 (d) above is required;

(iii) A supplement to the regular programme is required for special coaching in an academic subject taught by the educational institution to make up for deficiencies attributable to the child's change of schooling as a result of expatriation or a change of the staff member's official duty station, or for special coaching in an academic subject not included in the educational institution curriculum but required for the child's subsequent education;

(f) Enrolment and tuition expenses for an apprenticeship or other similar arrangement when the educational institution certifies that any work placement is an integral part of the full-time curriculum and on the condition that the child receives no salary or remuneration for services rendered;

(g) Enrolment and tuition expenses for summer courses when the educational institution certifies that such courses are a prerequisite for further attendance during the subsequent regular academic year and for the institution's regular diploma. When admissible, expenses for summer courses are reimbursed as part of the admissible expenses incurred for the prior academic year, subject to the maximum claim amount.[148]

The education grant is limited to $30,566 per child per academic year.[149]

148. *Id.*
149. *Id.*

Chapter 5

Often Overlooked Issues Pertaining to World Treaty Organization Pensions

5.1 Obtaining a Present Value of the Pension

A lawyer may consider obtaining a formal pension valuation in order to obtain a present value of the employee's pension. A pension valuation is a determination of the present value of a future stream of income. The purpose of such a task is to figure out in today's dollars, what is the value of all future payments to be received from the pension? The valuation itself is more of an art than a science, since it is based on many assumptions. The major assumptions include life expectancy, start date, interest rates, and tax discounts.

In order to obtain a sound pension valuation, the lawyer will need to engage an expert, such as an actuary or a certified public accountant. There may be others who have qualifications and training to qualify as an expert for this purpose. The pension value depends on what assumptions are used by the expert in the calculation, and as such each expert's calculation will likely be different.

Obtaining a pension valuation may be a good strategic decision in certain cases. For example, determining the present value of the pension could allow parties to compare its value with other assets, such as a house, so that parties could trade-off. It could also obviate the need or concern about preservation of a survivor benefit. Obtaining a pension valuation, while not rare, is not the normal course of action and can be a costly step. As such, it should only be done if a trade-off is being contemplated and not as a matter of course.

5.2 Remember the Survivor Annuity

As described in each chapter, these organizations have very specific rules relating to the award or designation of a survivor benefit. In each case dealing with one of these organizations it is helpful to refresh yourself for that organization's specific rules to ensure you are setting the right expectations for your client and protecting yourself from liability by giving accurate advice. Not only are these organizations particular, but they are also quite similar, so it is easy to confuse their rules.

Remember, some organizations allow a remarriage to override a beneficiary designation to a former spouse.[1] In those situations, it is important to analyze whether the participant is likely to remarry, or if the former spouse actually needs the security of the survivor benefit. This is an important consideration for where to put effort in negotiations and arguments in court. Additionally, if this is not the participant's first marriage, it will be important to determine if any such benefit was awarded to the prior spouse. For the organizations that have limits on the reductions a participant's benefit can absorb, if such limit is already reached, there may be little left to negotiate for.

In cases when a remarriage of the participant is likely and that remarriage will override the beneficiary designation, the other party may want to look at life insurance options to secure a future benefit.

5.3 Allocate the Cost of the Survivor Annuity Correctly

Each chapter about a specific organization discusses whether the plan can shift the cost of the survivor benefit. If it is not easily done, then there must be some sort of calculation done to determine that cost and reduce the appropriate party's share of the benefit accordingly. To be able to do any of this, it is important to determine each party's position on the issue early so that any necessary information can be gathered. Some of these organizations can run estimates of the benefit for the participant, which is a helpful tool if such a calculation needs to be done.

1. *See* Sections 1.6, 1.7, 2.6, 2.7, 3.6, 3.7, 4.12, 5.4 herein.

5.4 Advise the Client of the Effect of Remarriage

As a matter of professional liability, it is important to advise the client regarding the effect of their remarriage, or the remarriage of the participant. If a remarriage overrides a beneficiary designation to a former spouse, it is important the former spouse understands the possibility of losing that benefit and that there's nothing that can be done to prevent that. Similarly, if there is a restriction on the former spouse's remarriage as it relates to their benefits from these organizations, it is important the former spouse understands these restrictions. While there is nothing that can be done to change the plan's rules, the former spouse might adjust their behaviors to prevent a change in their entitlement to the benefits.

5.5 Resolve Before Employee Moves Away

A major consideration in cases where the participant is still actively employed is when does their current position agreement terminate, and whether they are eligible to move abroad easily. This concern is especially relevant when dealing with a participant who is not a citizen of the country that has jurisdiction over the divorce. If the participant leaves the country, then forcing the participant's participation in the process to execute an order dividing the pension after the divorce occurs can be incredibly difficult.

First, there is the issue of simply knowing where the participant is located. This information can probably be learned from the employing organization but may also make the participant available to disciplinary procedures internally for not cooperating with the divorce process.

Second, if the divorce matter has closed such that the participant must be served with process to reopen the case, then the rules of the country where the participant lives must be observed for proper service. Some countries participate in the Hague Service Convention. The Hague Service Convention is an international treaty that provides litigants who are citizens of member countries with the opportunity to serve legal documents to people, or parties, abroad.[2] The

2. Convention on the Service Abroad of Judicial and Extrajudicial Documents in Civil or Commercial Matters (Nov. 15, 1965).

Convention was put into effect on November 15, 1965. For member countries, the Convention is applicable in all civil or commercial cases in which it is necessary to serve a judicial or extrajudicial document internationally.[3] According to the text of the Convention, each member country is required to designate a central authority that undertakes and receives service requests from other countries.[4] If the document requested to be served complies with the provisions of the Convention, the central authority must then serve the document or have it served by the necessary agency.[5] Currently, there are 91 countries that are contracting parties to the Hague Service Convention.[6] In practice, the Hague Service Convention permits parties to proceed with litigation, even when the opposing party is in another country. Importantly, as it relates here, the Hague Service Convention does not prohibit service of judicial process by mail where it is otherwise an acceptable or permissible means of service.[7] As such, a country's central authority is not the only available means for service. Note, it may be necessary for a litigant to file a motion requesting permission to serve the other party by mail. The rules will vary in each case and are based on the countries involved.

Third, it might be easier to exercise jurisdiction over the participant by filing an enforcement action in their current location, but that may be incredibly inconvenient to the former spouse. More importantly than inconvenience, the laws of the participant's country may differ from the laws where the divorce was entered, so the ability to divide the pension may differ and change the benefit available to the former spouse. For a former spouse who is relying on a certain division of the retirement benefits a sudden change in the governing laws can be life changing.

Fourth, if the division of the pension must go through a different jurisdiction, then it is likely going to be more expensive for both parties, as they will likely both have to hire an attorney in that

3. *Id.* Art. 1.
4. *Id.* Art. 2.
5. *Id.* Art. 5.
6. HCCH, *HCCH Members*, https://www.hcch.net/en/states/hcch-members (last visited Feb. 16, 2024).
7. Water Splash, Inc. v. Menton, 137 S. Ct. 1504 (2017).

jurisdiction, and potentially maintain their divorce attorney to ensure the division going forward in the participant's jurisdiction is as close as possible to the division agreed upon or ordered in their divorce.

5.6 Knowing the "Maximum Survivor Annuity"

In general, these plans have a survivor annuity that they are able to provide to the named or eligible beneficiaries. While the plans do not publish what they consider to be the "maximum survivor annuity," for some of them it may be less than 100 percent of the participant's full annuity, and for others it may be the employee's full annuity. If the agreement says the former spouse shall receive the full or maximum survivor annuity, and the plan allows for up to 100 percent of the employee annuity, the parties could be creating a financial situation they did not intend. Specifically, the parties could create a scenario wherein the funds paid out during the participant's retirement years is substantially reduced, and the former spouse receives a windfall upon the participant's death.

To avoid providing a benefit amount that the parties do not intend, it is important that the drafting of the court order, divorce decree, and settlement agreement are all clear and specific in their description of the award to the former spouse. Clearly stating a 50 percent or 100 percent survivor benefit, or describing the survivor benefit as a dollar amount, is preferable to stating "maximum."

5.7 Timely Entry of the Court Order Dividing the Benefit/Posthumous Orders

The order dividing the retirement benefit (or any other benefit for that matter) should be executed by the parties ideally at the same time as any agreement. If not, then as soon as possible thereafter so it can be submitted to the court to process with the divorce decree. The longer the delay, the higher the chances are that the former spouse will lose the benefit they negotiated for or were awarded.

The participant could die in the period between the divorce and the retirement order being drafted, submitted, or accepted by the plan. Some states have made determinations on how to handle these situations. New York found that a former spouse who had received death benefits due to being listed as beneficiary on a defined contribution account had to return the funds received to the estate of her former husband (participant) because she had waived such interest in the settlement agreement.[8] In making such a finding though, the court stated that the plan administrator did nothing wrong because it had simply followed the beneficiary designation that was on file at the time it was notified of the participant's death.[9] This situation poses a problem for the estate of the deceased participant, being that if the former spouse who improperly receives funds and subsequently disappears, the estate may not have means to track the former spouse and recover the funds.

What about getting an order filed nunc pro tunc, so that even if it is actually entered after the participant's death, its effective date is prior to the participant's death? States and federal circuits within the United States do not agree on how to handle this very situation. Although these organizations are not subject to the QDRO rules of ERISA, if a state has not yet made a decision here it may look to its federal counterpart for guidance, so it is still relevant information.

On a federal circuit level, only the First and Fourth Circuits have rejected post-humous QDROs.[10] The First Circuit's opinion was per curiam and simply supported the decision of the plan to reject the

---

8. *In the Matter of the Estate of Daniel Kelly, Deceased*, 950 N.Y.S.2d 415, 36 Misc. 3d 736 (N.Y. 2012). Finding that even though the participant had died without changing his beneficiary designation, the settlement agreement specifically stated that preexisting beneficiary designations were void as of the date of divorce, and the parties each waived interested in the other's retirement interests, therefore, the former spouse who received the beneficiary payment had to return the funds to be distributed through the estate. Texas made a similar ruling in *Smalley v. Smalley*, 399 S.W.3d 631 (Tex. 2013) and included an analysis of the federal regulations surrounding retirement plans administered by the federal government, which are similarly not governed by ERISA but made analogies to ERISA reasoning.

9. *Id.*

10. The term "QDRO" in this section is used broadly. As it relates to the cases referenced in the appellate courts, those cases involved QDROs. However, as it relates to the orders described in this book, use of the term "QDRO" in the specific would result in a rejection. As such, the use here is in reference to any domestic relations order dividing a retirement benefit, whether under the name QDRO, Order for Spousal Support, Retirement Benefit Court Order, or otherwise.

order for other flaws. In fact, the case specifically states that it does not determine the question of if it would enforce a proper posthumous QDRO.[11] The Fourth Circuit, however, specifically states that a survivor's interest vests in any survivor benefit as of the participant's death.[12] Therefore, if no interest was awarded or designated as of the participant's death, no survivor benefit is payable to such person. Thus while the parties may have agreed that one party would receive a survivor benefit from the other's pension, without securing it via court order or beneficiary designation form in the Fourth Circuit, the agreement is of little help. Therefore, in cases where a survivor benefit is awarded, it is incredibly important to get the court order and beneficiary designation filed promptly.

To the contrary, the Second, Third, Fifth, and Tenth Circuits have all decided that simply because a QDRO may be issued after the participant's death does not make the QDRO moot. Instead, because ERISA allows for an 18-month period for a QDRO to be revised after it is rejected, a QDRO must be acceptable within that time period, regardless of the participant's death.[13] Alternatively, these circuits state that the QDRO is the most effective enforcement tool for an otherwise valid divorce agreement or order, and there is no reason why it must be completed prior to the benefits being payable on the account of the participant's retirement or death.[14]

The Sixth, Seventh, Eighth, and Twelfth Circuits have not yet opined on this matter.

First, a lawyer should research to see if their state has opined on the issue of a posthumous retirement division order, if it is an issue in their case. If not, then the federal circuit's opinion will be persuasive, but not binding, on the state court's decision. A judge not otherwise trained in retirement orders and the complexities of implementing an order after the participant's death may not think twice about signing off. However, a judge that understands the payment schemes and

---

11. Garcia-Tatupu v. Bell, 747 Fed. Appx. 873 (2019), affirming lower court decision Garcia-Tatupu v. Bell, 296 F. Supp. 3d, 407 (D. Mass. 2017).

12. Hopkins v. AT&T Global Info. Solutions Co., 105 F.3d 153 (1997).

13. Patton v. Denver Post Corp., 326 F.3d 1148, 1151 (2003).

14. Trs. of the Dirs. Guild of America-Producer Pension Benefits Plans v. Tise, 234 F.3d 415, 421 (2000).

potential to pay out benefits in excess of what the participant had earned if signing a posthumous retirement benefit court order may not be so willing to do so.

5.8 Commuted Benefit and Timing Thereof

As described within each organization's chapter, these pensions allow a participant to take a lump sum from their pension benefit. And, as described within each organization's section, no court order can require the participant to commute any amount of the benefit—they can only require that if a benefit is commuted, that a certain amount be paid directly from the plan to the former spouse.

Timing of the commuted benefit, language in the separation agreement or divorce decree, and drafting and submission of any court order to the plan is key, especially if the participant is not cooperating. For example, if the participant retires immediately after the divorce is final, but before the court order is accepted by the plan then the participant has a window of time available to them to commute a benefit and not have a portion be paid directly to the former spouse.

In this scenario, if the language in the separation agreement or divorce decree is not clear that the former spouse has an entitlement to a portion of any commuted benefit then it's possible that the participant could keep the entire commuted benefit for themselves, leaving the former spouse with a smaller portion of the monthly annuity payments.

Alternatively, if the participant quickly spends the commuted benefit, then the former spouse might have a hard time recovering their share of the benefit, even if the separation agreement or divorce decree language clearly entitles the former spouse to a portion thereof.

The notion of a noncooperative participant is not just for a person acting in bad faith to prevent their former spouse from receiving a portion of commuted benefits. Many times parties simply do not get these court orders completed immediately following their divorce and innocently assume that everything has been taken care of by their lawyers or the other party. Then, when an issue arises years later they are genuinely surprised that the retirement order is yet to be resolved. In these circumstances, a participant may have spent the commuted benefit truly believing they were receiving only their share, and then may have become accustomed to a certain lifestyle based on the amount of annuity they are receiving. Understandably, they would be upset to learn their income is about to decrease and based on jurisdiction they might owe arrears for the annuity payments they received to their former spouse.

These are all avoidable situations if the retirement order is prepared at the time of the agreement/trial and submitted to the court at the time of the divorce hearing or immediately thereafter.

Chapter 6

Litigation Considerations

6.1 How to Determine Income

The first task when analyzing the income of an employee of an intergovernmental organization is to determine whether they are being paid on a net or gross basis. If they are paid on a net basis then it is important to understand the jurisdiction's rules regarding grossing up income for support purposes. See Section 6.2.2 herein for more information. In addition, if paid on a net basis and the employee receives a tax allowance, is that tax allowance considered income in the jurisdiction?

Employees may also receive other allowances and subsidies from the organization. It will be important to receive a record of all income the employee receives from the organization and for what purpose. For example, some employees receive an allowance for a spouse who cannot work in the duty country. Whether that allowance is considered income is one thing, but whether it matters going forward is another. The employee will lose that allowance following the divorce, so those funds should not be considered in determining future income for support purposes.

Each jurisdiction has unique considerations of income for support purposes, and these organizations provide substantial additional benefits to their employees. Getting the income amount right will be key for a proper support award.

6.2 Taxation

Whether an employee's compensation from an international organization will be taxed at the federal, state, and/or local level is based on the person's citizenship, immigration status, and specific international organization employer. While a consultation with a tax attorney may be necessary to fully understand the impact on your client and their situation, the following information is general and is provided to help identify issues you may need to look into further.

Any exemption from taxation a person received due to their being employed by an international organization is limited to the compensation received from that organization for official acts *during the period of employment.*[1] This distinction means that pension and retirement benefits received by a former international organization employee will be taxed as retirement income, even if their compensation during employment was not.[2]

The person's immigration and/or citizenship status is also important here. U.S. citizens are not exempt from paying taxes on compensation from international organization employers, neither are foreign employees who have signed a waiver in furtherance of their efforts to obtain permanent resident status (a "green card"), depending on which international organization is their employer.[3] For example, the articles of agreement for both the IMF and the World Bank provide that foreign employees are exempt from U.S. tax laws.[4] If the taxability of a person's income is important to your case, it is critical to discuss with a tax attorney.

6.2.1 Taxation and Determining Child Support (and Spousal Support)

If one or both of the parties is not a U.S. citizen or otherwise does not have their income taxed, it could present an interesting question as it relates to the determination of child support. Some states determine child support based on the gross income of the parents. Where both parents pay income tax, or both do not, then the impact of the state's child support calculation on each party is equal.

---

1. Internal Revenue Service, Employees of Foreign Governments or International Organizations.

2. See each chapter herein for specifics related to each organization. Some of the organizations discussed herein provide an additional payment to their former employees to cover the national taxes due on pension benefits.

3. Internal Revenue Service, *supra* note 1.

4. *Id.*

However, for states that use gross income to calculate child support obligations, and one party does not have their income taxed and one party does, it creates an interesting question as to what, if anything, the court will do to equalize the impact of the calculation on each parent. One idea is to "gross up" the nontaxed parent's income by treating their actual income as "net" and then adding a fictional amount to create an increased "gross" amount so that the income for each parent at least in relation to tax payments is treated similarly.

Some states have determined that this is inappropriate based on their domestic relations laws. Maryland, for example, states that "actual income" will be considered for purposes of calculating child support.[5] The only exception is if a party has been found to be voluntarily impoverished, then that party's income may be increased. To the contrary, the District of Columbia's code section specifically states that child support will be calculated using a party's gross income, which includes "[t]axes paid on a party's income by an employer or, if the income is nontaxable, the amount of taxes that would be paid if the income were taxable."[6]

While at the time of publishing the tax laws in the United States are such that spousal support is not deductible from the payor nor taxable to the payee, that law is scheduled to sunset in 2025. Without a renewal by Congress, the taxability of spousal support may again be shiftable between the parties and addressed as a part of settlement negotiations.

6.2.2 Taxation of Life Insurance Proceeds

In the United States, life insurance proceeds are generally not taxable to the recipient.[7] This is not the case in all countries. As such, if the former spouse in your case is going to be named the beneficiary of a life insurance policy and is not a U.S. citizen or intends to leave the United States after the divorce, the attorney should consult with an attorney where the former spouse intends to relocate to see if anything can be done to avoid or limit the taxes the former spouse may otherwise owe if they receive the proceeds directly. Instruments such as a life insurance trust may be helpful tools.

---

5. Lemley v. Lemley, 649 A.2d 1119, 1131–32 (Md. App. 1994).
6. D.C. Code § 16-916.01(d)(1)(X).
7. I.R.C. § 101(1)(1).

6.3 Clarity of Awards

It is important to know your state's approach to pension language. For example, if a court awards a former spouse "50 percent of the marital share of the pension" what exactly does that include?[8] When litigating a case that involves the division of a pension it may be best to submit a proposed Judgment of Divorce, or Findings of Fact to help guide the judge to address each element of the pension, so nothing is vague.

Most importantly, does the "50 percent of the marital share of the pension" language include survivor benefits? If so, how will the reduction required for the survivor benefit be handled? Although none of the pension systems described herein allow for the reduction to be shifted between the parties via a court order or the beneficiary form, that does not mean a shift cannot happen. The parties merely need to enter into one order immediately after the divorce is entered and have the participant submit the beneficiary designation form to secure the benefit. Then, once the participant retires and commences benefits, the parties enter into a new court order, which merely properly adjusts the amount payable to the former spouse to allocate the reduction where the parties want it. While this is not ideal in that the issue is not resolved once and for all at the time of divorce, it is at least a means to accomplish the goal.

Another consideration with the language "50 percent of the marital share" is whether that includes costs-of-living adjustments on the payment to the former spouse.

And, as it relates to these plans in particular, is this language meant to include both monthly and lump-sum payments, or only one or the other? It most likely does include both forms of payment, though these plans do require a specific statement for each benefit form to be sure they are making the correct payment to the former spouse.

---

8. McCoy v. Feinman, 99 N.Y.2d 297 (2002) citing *Majauskas v. Majauskas*, 61 N.Y.2d 481 (1984), which states that for New York a mere reference to divide retirement benefits is not a clear showing of intent to divide the survivor benefit. Pleasant v. Pleasant, 632 A.2d 202 (Md. 1993) finding that "the right to a survivor annuity is incident to the marital relationship, and that such a right analogous to the right to pension benefits themselves, falls with the definition of marital property[.]".

6.4 Earnings Withholding Orders

Pursuant to the International Organizations Immunities Act,[9] these organizations have immunity from earnings withholding orders, because they are not orders relating to the organization's commercial activity. Further, to require such adherence in the United States would require the same adherence in all member countries for each organization, which would be a large administrative burden that would impact the ability of the organization to perform its key functions, and as such could render the organization incapable.[10]

However, each organization here will comply in some fashion to provide a spouse or former spouse with financial support from the participant/employee's salary. Section 3.12 herein describes the steps necessary and internal rules of the World Bank. With respect to the IMF, its Code of Conduct, states:

> It is not the Fund's role to determine whether local laws have been violated by a staff member, as that is for the domestic courts to decide. However, if the Fund receives a lawful order from a court or other governmental authority instructing it to withhold an amount of salary to be paid to a staff member to satisfy an outstanding legal obligation, the Fund will not allow the staff member to take undue advantage of the fact that it is immune from such orders.[11]

While the information available to the public does not explicitly state that the IMF will honor such an order, the Code of Conduct does imply that the IMF will encourage the staff member to make payment directly or will make payment to the former spouse directly if the staff member continues to fail to make the legal support payments.

---

9. 22 U.S.C. §§ 288 *et seq.*

10. Atkinson v. Inter-American Dev. Bank, et al., 156 F.3d 1335 (D.C. Cir. 1998).

11. Mr. P (No. 2) v. Int'l Monetary Fund, IMF Tribunal Judgment No. 2001-2 (Nov. 20, 2001) citing the IMF Code of Conduct.

6.5 Access to Employee Information

How to request information about an employee's salary, pension benefit, or other benefits directly from each institution is described within each organization's chapter herein. For retirees of these organizations, it is important to remember that they are not required to submit information to the IRS for national taxes. Some of these organizations may not provide a form 1099-R for their retirees receiving their pension benefits. However, an employee can still obtain a statement from the organization that provides the same information.

6.6 Multiple Divorce Decrees

Since these employees and their spouses may be citizens of countries other than the United States, they may be able to use the legal systems of other countries to obtain a divorce. As international organizations, none of the organizations described herein will prefer one of their member states' legal procedures over another. However, there may be conflicting decrees if a divorce is pending in one country, but a party rushes off to another country to obtain a divorce that may be more beneficial to them in terms of property division.

The IMF Tribunal decided a case in which a wife was pursuing a divorce from her husband, the IMF employee. Amid the Maryland divorce proceedings, the husband went to Egypt and obtained a divorce, without any notice to or participation of wife. The IMF Tribunal described the Egyptian divorce as paperwork with a notary, with a two-month ability to rescind the paperwork to reconcile the marriage. If he did not rescind the paperwork, the divorce would be final, with no property division between the parties.[12] After the Egyptian divorce became final, the Maryland Court issued its decision that awarded the wife a portion of the husband's IMF pension. The question presented was whether Maryland even had jurisdiction to enter its divorce order since the parties were already divorced under Egyptian law. The IMF Tribunal reports that Maryland held it had jurisdiction to enter its order because it had jurisdiction to divide

12. Mr. P. (No. 2) v. Int'l Monetary Fund, Judgment No. 2001-2 (Nov. 20, 2001).

marital assets that were not addressed by the Egyptian divorce and over which it had jurisdiction as being assets located within the state. As such, the IMF Tribunal found that both the Egyptian divorce and the Maryland property division order were valid, and the wife was therefore entitled to the portion of the IMF pension awarded by the Maryland court following the Egyptian divorce.[13]

Even in cases such as the preceding, it is important to do as much as possible in each jurisdiction to further a party's position. For example, the former spouse should take steps to have a court order dividing the benefits entered so that if the IMF accepts that jurisdiction's decision, then the former spouse is already set up for success.

13. *Id.*

Chapter 7

Sample Language and Settlement Considerations

7.1 Separation Agreements

To divide a pension benefit, including cost of living adjustments (both monthly benefits and any commuted amount, or withdrawal benefit):

> *Alex is an employee of the [Organization] and is entitled to benefits from the [Retirement Plan]. The parties agree that Shane will receive 50% of the marital share of any benefits Alex receives from the [Retirement Plan], whether it be a withdrawal benefit, commuted lump-sum, monthly pension benefit, or otherwise. Shane's share shall also be adjusted to include a pro rata share of any cost-of-living adjustments applied thereto.*

To divide a pension benefit only, and prohibit commuted benefits:

> *Ronald is an employee of the [Organization] and is entitled to benefits from the [Retirement Plan]. The parties agree that Florence will receive 50% of the marital share of any monthly pension benefits Ronald receives from the [Retirement Plan]. Florence's share shall also be adjusted to include a pro rata share of any cost-of-living adjustments applied thereto. The parties agree that Ronald shall not withdraw his interest in the [Retirement Plan]. The parties further agree that Ronald shall not commute any amount of his [Retirement Plan] benefit.*

***A word of caution here. The prohibition against commuting any of the benefits cannot be enforced against any of the plans described herein, and once elected and paid out cannot be undone. If choosing this option, it is also best to include language in the court order that the former spouse (Florence) will receive a share of all benefits (inclusive of commuted benefits). Otherwise, the participant, Ronald, could commute a portion and Florence would not receive a share of the commuted lump sum.*

PRACTICE TIP

The prohibition against commuting any of the benefits cannot be enforced against any of the plans discussed herein. Once elected and paid out, the commutation cannot be undone.

To divide only commuted benefits:

Lucky is an employee of the [Organization] and is entitled to benefits from the [Retirement Plan]. The parties agree that Lucky will elect to commute a portion of her SRP into a lump sum, and that Albert shall receive $25,000 of said commuted lump sum. Albert shall not be entitled to any other benefits from Lucky's [Retirement Plan] to include monthly pension benefits or a survivor benefit.

***A word of caution here. If Lucky chooses not to file the election form to receive a commuted lump-sum benefit, then Albert will not receive any benefit from the [Retirement Plan]. Additional language should be included to protect Albert's interest so he can recover from a different asset, if necessary. For example: In the event Lucky does not elect to receive a lump sum benefit, or Albert receives less than $25,000 from the lump sum benefit, Lucky shall pay to Albert $25,000 within ten (10) days of the date she begins to receive benefits from her SRP.*

To provide a waiver of interest:

Rhiannon hereby waives any and all interest she may have in Jillian's [Retirement Plan], including any monthly pension benefit, commuted lump sum, or survivor benefits. Such waiver shall be effective as of the date of this Agreement, and Jillian shall be responsible for sharing this Agreement with the Organization to prevent the payment of any [Retirement Plan] or survivor benefit from being paid to Rhiannon. Rhiannon shall cooperate with Jillian's efforts and execute any forms requested by the Organization to effectuate this paragraph.

To provide for a survivor benefit:

The parties intend that Dave shall receive a 50% survivor benefit from Jennifer's [Retirement Plan]. Within ten (10) days of the date of this Agreement Jennifer shall complete and submit the requisite paperwork to the Benefit Administrator to elect such survivor benefit for Dave and provide him with proof thereof. Dave may request no more than once per year that Jennifer confirm this election has not been revoked, and may demand proof thereof. The parties acknowledge that this survivor benefit cannot be secured through a court order submitted to the [Organization].

***A note of caution here. The election to divide the pension and create the survivor pension has to be on file at the time Jennifer would begin to receive pension benefits. If it is not, then the plan may not create a survivor pension for Dave—please check the organization's rules to see what the plan in your case will allow. Additional language should be included to protect Dave's interest, such as:*

In the event Jennifer fails to file the election to create the survivor pension for Dave prior to her beginning to receive benefits, Jennifer shall name Dave as beneficiary of a life insurance policy in the amount of [insert a sum certain] and Jennifer shall be responsible for maintaining such policy through the first of Dave or Jennifer to die.

To provide for a beneficiary designation:

The parties agree that Liz shall designate Charlene as her sole beneficiary of her interest in the [Retirement Plan]. Charlene acknowledges that in the event Liz remarries that the Plan will pay certain benefits to Liz's then-current spouse that may result in a reduction or complete bar of benefits payable to Charlene. Charlene shall not have any action against Liz or her then-current spouse in such an event.

To divide any disability pension:

In the event Calvin retires and is receiving a disability pension, the parties agree that Jolene will receive a 50% marital share of such disability pension. Jolene's 50% marital share of such disability pension shall continue to be paid until for so long as the disability pension payments are made to Calvin. In the event the disability pension converts to a normal pension at any time, Jolene shall receive her 50% marital share of such normal pension.

7.2 Delaying Divorce

Parties may agree to delay filing for their divorce once they have reached agreement on all issues. Popular reasons include the following:

- If it is near the end of the participant's employment term, the employer may pay to relocate the family back to their home country, thereby saving the family certain moving expenses.
- It may be near the period when the employee will receive an allowance to return to the home country for a visit, and the parties may decide to use such funds to move the former spouse and/or children to the home country.
- The spouse may lose their ability to remain in the United States (especially if via visa) and the parties not want the spouse to be required to leave the U.S. yet.

- The spouse may be obtaining a different visa to be able to remain in the U.S. but needs additional time to secure the new visa.
- They may have agreed to wait until a child reaches a certain age or part of the school year.

However, it is important to remember that an agreement to delay filing for divorce may not be enforceable. If a person meets the elements to file for divorce in their jurisdiction, then they may do so at any time. Moreover, with the growing trend in the country to include or have exclusively non-fault grounds for divorce, it is becoming increasingly easy to sever the bonds of marriage. Therefore, it is important to explain this to your client, and potentially include a damages clause into the agreement if one party files for divorce before the intended date. For example, if the parties are waiting to divorce because the spouse can earn more working in the United States and they want to allow the spouse to increase their savings, perhaps the damages clause is that if the participant files early, they have to make a lump-sum payment to the spouse. However, in this scenario, if the spouse filed early they would not receive a payment from the employee because the reason for delaying the divorce was to benefit the spouse.

Of course, just as the parties may agree to delay filing for divorce, either party may frustrate such agreement. The biggest issue is that if the employee files early and the spouse loses their visa, the spouse must return to the home country. This action could cause custody issues, especially if the children remain with the employee to finish out the school year, but the intent was for the children to return to the home country with the spouse.

Appendix 1

WBG SRP, Article 26, Schedule B, Tables 2A and 2B

Table 2A: Survivor Annuity Factors for Participants Hired Before December 31, 2015

Amount of Survivor Annuity as Percentage of Retired Participant's Pension

Retired Participant's Age	Age Difference Between Retired Participant and Beneficiary										
	Retired Participant Older than Beneficiary					Age Difference Less Than or Equal 5 Years	Retired Participant Younger than Beneficiary				
	10	9	8	7	6		6	7	8	9	10
50	32.1%	33.0%	34.0%	35.0%	36.1%	37.2%	38.5%	39.8%	41.2%	42.7%	44.3%
51	32.7%	33.7%	34.7%	35.7%	36.8%	38.0%	39.3%	40.7%	42.2%	43.8%	45.5%
52	33.3%	34.3%	35.4%	36.5%	37.6%	38.9%	40.2%	41.7%	43.2%	44.9%	46.7%
53	34.0%	35.0%	36.1%	37.2%	38.5%	39.8%	41.2%	42.7%	44.3%	46.1%	47.9%
54	34.7%	35.7%	36.8%	38.0%	39.3%	40.7%	42.2%	43.8%	45.5%	47.3%	49.3%
55	35.4%	36.5%	37.6%	38.9%	40.2%	41.7%	43.2%	44.9%	46.7%	48.6%	50.7%
56	36.1%	37.2%	38.5%	39.8%	41.2%	42.7%	44.3%	46.1%	47.9%	50.0%	52.2%
57	36.8%	38.0%	39.3%	40.7%	42.2%	43.8%	45.5%	47.3%	49.3%	51.5%	53.8%
58	37.6%	38.9%	40.2%	41.7%	43.2%	44.9%	46.7%	48.6%	50.7%	53.0%	55.6%
59	38.5%	39.8%	41.2%	42.7%	44.3%	46.1%	47.9%	50.0%	52.2%	54.7%	57.4%
60	39.3%	40.7%	42.2%	43.8%	45.5%	47.3%	49.3%	51.5%	53.8%	56.5%	59.3%
61	40.2%	41.7%	43.2%	44.9%	46.7%	48.6%	50.7%	53.0%	55.6%	58.3%	61.4%
62	41.2%	42.7%	44.3%	46.1%	47.9%	50.0%	52.2%	54.7%	57.4%	60.3%	63.6%
63	42.2%	43.8%	45.5%	47.3%	49.3%	51.5%	53.8%	56.5%	59.3%	62.5%	66.0%
64	43.2%	44.9%	46.7%	48.6%	50.7%	53.0%	55.6%	58.3%	61.4%	64.8%	68.6%
65	44.3%	46.1%	47.9%	50.0%	52.2%	54.7%	57.4%	60.3%	63.6%	67.3%	71.4%
66	45.5%	47.3%	49.3%	51.5%	53.8%	56.5%	59.3%	62.5%	66.0%	70.0%	74.5%
67	46.7%	48.6%	50.7%	53.0%	55.6%	58.3%	61.4%	64.8%	68.6%	72.9%	77.8%
68	47.9%	50.0%	52.2%	54.7%	57.4%	60.3%	63.6%	67.3%	71.4%	76.1%	81.4%
69	49.3%	51.5%	53.8%	56.5%	59.3%	62.5%	66.0%	70.0%	74.5%	79.5%	85.4%
70	50.7%	53.0%	55.6%	58.3%	61.4%	64.8%	68.6%	72.9%	77.8%	83.3%	89.7%

Table 2B. Survivor Annuity Factors for Participants Hired on or After December 31, 2015

Age Difference Between Retired Participant and Beneficiary										
Retired Participant Older than Beneficiary					Age Difference Less than or Equal 5 years	Retired Participant Younger than Beneficiary				
10	9	8	7	6		6	7	8	9	10
41.2%	42.7%	44.3%	46.1%	47.9%	50.0%	52.2%	54.7%	57.4%	60.3%	63.6%

Appendix 2

WBG Pension Reduction Factors to Provide Greater Survivor Pensions

Table 4A. Pension Reduction Factors for Participants Hired Before December 31, 2015

Amount of Reduction in Retired Participant's Pension to Provide a Survivor Annuity of 100% of Retired Participant's Reduced Pension

Retired Participant's Age	Age Difference Between Retirement Participant and Beneficiary										
	Retired Participant Older than Beneficiary					Age Difference Less Than or Equal 5 Years	Retired Participant Younger than Beneficiary				
	10	9	8	7	6		6	7	8	9	10
50	14.8%	14.2%	13.6%	13.0%	12.4%	11.8%	11.2%	10.6%	10.0%	9.4%	8.8%
51	14.4%	13.8%	13.2%	12.6%	12.0%	11.4%	10.8%	10.2%	9.6%	9.0%	8.4%
52	14.0%	13.4%	12.6%	12.2%	11.6%	11.0%	10.4%	9.8%	9.2%	8.6%	8.0%
53	13.6%	13.0%	12.4%	11.8%	11.2%	10.6%	10.0%	9.4%	8.8%	8.2%	7.6%
54	13.2%	12.6%	12.0%	11.4%	10.8%	10.2%	9.6%	9.0%	8.4%	7.8%	7.2%
55	12.6%	12.2%	11.6%	11.0%	10.4%	9.8%	9.2%	8.6%	8.0%	7.4%	6.8%
56	12.4%	11.8%	11.2%	10.6%	10.0%	9.4%	8.8%	8.2%	7.6%	7.0%	6.4%
57	12.0%	11.4%	10.8%	10.2%	9.6%	9.0%	8.4%	7.8%	7.2%	6.6%	6.0%
58	11.6%	11.0%	10.4%	9.8%	9.2%	8.6%	8.0%	7.4%	6.8%	6.2%	5.6%
59	11.2%	10.6%	10.0%	9.4%	8.8%	8.2%	7.6%	7.0%	6.4%	5.8%	5.2%
60	10.8%	10.2%	9.6%	9.0%	8.4%	7.8%	7.2%	6.6%	6.0%	5.4%	4.8%
61	10.4%	9.8%	9.2%	8.6%	8.0%	7.4%	6.8%	6.2%	5.6%	5.0%	4.4%
62	10.0%	9.4%	8.8%	8.2%	7.6%	7.0%	6.4%	5.8%	5.2%	4.6%	4.0%
63	9.6%	9.0%	8.4%	7.8%	7.2%	6.6%	6.0%	5.4%	4.8%	4.2%	3.6%
64	9.2%	8.6%	8.0%	7.4%	6.8%	6.2%	5.6%	5.0%	4.4%	3.8%	3.2%
65	8.8%	8.2%	7.6%	7.0%	6.4%	5.8%	5.2%	4.6%	4.0%	3.4%	2.8%
66	8.4%	7.8%	7.2%	6.6%	6.0%	5.4%	4.8%	4.2%	3.6%	3.0%	2.4%
67	8.0%	7.4%	6.8%	6.2%	5.6%	5.0%	4.4%	3.8%	3.2%	2.6%	2.0%
68	7.6%	7.0%	6.4%	5.8%	5.2%	4.6%	4.0%	3.4%	2.8%	2.2%	1.6%
69	7.2%	6.6%	6.0%	5.4%	4.8%	4.2%	3.6%	3.0%	2.4%	1.8%	1.2%
70	6.8%	6.2%	5.6%	5.0%	4.4%	3.8%	3.2%	2.6%	2.0%	1.4%	0.8%

Amount of Reduction in Retired Participant's Pension to Provide a Survivor Annuity of 50% of Retired Participant's Reduced Pension

Retired Participant's Age	Age Difference Between Retirement Participant and Beneficiary										
	Retired Participant Older than Beneficiary					Age Difference Less Than or Equal 5 Years	Retired Participant Younger than Beneficiary				
	10	9	8	7	6		6	7	8	9	10
50	3.9%	3.6%	3.3%	3.0%	2.7%	2.4%	2.1%	1.8%	1.5%	1.2%	0.9%
51	3.7%	3.4%	3.1%	2.8%	2.5%	2.2%	1.9%	1.6%	1.3%	1.0%	0.7%
52	3.5%	3.2%	2.9%	2.6%	2.3%	2.0%	1.7%	1.4%	1.1%	0.8%	0.5%
53	3.3%	3.0%	2.7%	2.4%	2.1%	1.8%	1.5%	1.3%	0.9%	0.6%	0.3%
54	3.1%	2.8%	2.5%	2.2%	1.9%	1.6%	1.3%	1.0%	0.7%	0.4%	0.1%
55	2.9%	2.6%	2.3%	2.0%	1.7%	1.4%	1.1%	0.8%	0.5%	0.2%	0.0%
56	2.7%	2.4%	2.1%	1.8%	1.5%	1.2%	0.9%	0.6%	0.3%	0.0%	0.0%
57	2.5%	2.2%	1.9%	1.6%	1.3%	1.0%	0.7%	0.4%	0.1%	0.0%	0.0%
58	2.3%	2.0%	1.7%	1.4%	1.1%	0.8%	0.5%	0.2%	0.0%	0.0%	0.0%
59	2.1%	1.8%	1.5%	1.2%	0.9%	0.6%	0.3%	0.0%	0.0%	0.0%	0.0%
60	1.9%	1.6%	1.3%	1.0%	0.7%	0.4%	0.1%	0.0%	0.0%	0.0%	0.0%
61	1.7%	1.4%	1.1%	0.8%	0.5%	0.2%	0.0%	0.0%	0.0%	0.0%	0.0%
62	1.5%	1.2%	0.9%	0.6%	0.3%	0.0%	0.0%	0.0%	0.0%	0.0%	0.0%
63	1.3%	1.0%	0.7%	0.4%	0.1%	0.0%	0.0%	0.0%	0.0%	0.0%	0.0%
64	1.1%	0.8%	0.5%	0.2%	0.0%	0.0%	0.0%	0.0%	0.0%	0.0%	0.0%
65	0.9%	0.6%	0.3%	0.0%	0.0%	0.0%	0.0%	0.0%	0.0%	0.0%	0.0%
66	0.7%	0.4%	0.1%	0.0%	0.0%	0.0%	0.0%	0.0%	0.0%	0.0%	0.0%
67	0.5%	0.2%	0.0%	0.0%	0.0%	0.0%	0.0%	0.0%	0.0%	0.0%	0.0%
68	0.3%	0.0%	0.0%	0.0%	0.0%	0.0%	0.0%	0.0%	0.0%	0.0%	0.0%
69	0.1%	0.0%	0.0%	0.0%	0.0%	0.0%	0.0%	0.0%	0.0%	0.0%	0.0%
70	0.0%	0.0%	0.0%	0.0%	0.0%	0.0%	0.0%	0.0%	0.0%	0.0%	0.0%

Table 4B: Pension Reduction Factors for Participants Hired on or After December 31, 2015

Amount of Reduction in Retired Participant's Pension to Provide a Survivor Annuity of 100% of Retired Participant's Reduced Pension

Age difference Between Retired Participant and Beneficairy										
Retired Participant Older than Beneficiary					Age Difference Less Than or Equal 5 Years	Retired Participant Younger than Beneficiary				
10	9	8	7	6		6	7	8	9	10
10.0%	9.4%	8.8%	8.2%	7.6%	7.0%	6.4%	5.8%	5.2%	4.6%	4.0%

Amount of Reduction in Retired Participant's Pension to Provide a Survivor Annuity of 50% of Retired Participant's Reduced Pension

Age difference Between Retired Participant and Beneficairy										
Retired Participant Older than Beneficiary					Age Difference Less Than or Equal 5 Years	Retired Participant Younger than Beneficiary				
10	9	8	7	6		6	7	8	9	10
1.5%	1.2%	0.9%	0.6%	0.3%	0.0%	0.0%	0.0%	0.0%	0.0%	0.0%

Appendix 3

World Bank Education Reimbursable and Non-Reimbursable Expenses

Reimbursable

Application fee

Art fee

Boarding, if the school is not in the duty country

Building fee

Capital levy fee

Computer fee

Computer network cards, if required

Computer software that is required for a class

Development fee

Differential fee

Diploma fee

Enrollment fee

Exam fees (including PSAT, SAT, AP, TOEFL, GRE, baccalaureate)

Graduation fee

Lab fee

Levy certificate to reserve a seat (only for the Jakarta International School)

Physical plant fee

Registration Fee

Room and board, if school is not in duty country

School equipment/maintenance fee

Student fee

Summer school (university level only, and only if at same institution as regular school year)

Technology fee for in-classroom usage, not for dorm use

Non-Reimbursable

Activity fee

Before/after-care expenses

Boarding, if the school is in the duty country

Book not required for class, such as test prep books

Camp fees

Camping fee

Capital levy certificates to hold a seat at the school

Church fees

Class dues

Clothing

Cognitive testing

Computer connectivity costs (DSL line, high speed internet)

Computers and accessories

Date and voice connectivity fee

Dental expenses that would be covered under the medical insurance plan

Driver education fee

Early arrival fee

Equipment

Fax costs

Field trips (even if mandatory)

Fitness center fees

Fundraising

Haircuts

Handbooks

Health club fees

Installment plan fees

Instruction fees

Insurance refund plan

Interest charged

Jackets

Laptop computers and accessories (including modems, etc.)

Locker fees

Lunch fees

Meals

Medical testing or expenses that would be covered under the bank's medical insurance plan

Musical instruments

Postage

Prep courses for standardized tests

Prescription drugs

Psychological testing

PTA dues

Publication fees

Recital fees

Reservation fees

Retreat fees

Rings

Room and board, if the school is in the duty country

School supplies

Shipping and handling fees for books purchased online

Sports fees

Summer school (if not at the same university as regularly attended)

Summer school (kindergarten, primary and secondary school)

Taxes

Telephone charges

Transcript fees

Transportation fees

Uniforms

Visa fees

Voice and connectivity fees

Yearbooks

Appendix 4

Medical Insurance (MIP) Continuation (World Bank)

The World Bank Group
HR Operations
(202) 473-2222

International Bank for Reconstruction and Development
MSN G2-202
(202) 522-2150 fax

International Development Association
Washington, DC 20433 USA
hroperations@worldbankgroup.org

TO WHOM IT MAY CONCERN:
This fact sheet describes the options available to spouses and other eligible dependents of World Bank Group staff or retirees under the World Bank Group's Medical Insurance Plan (MIP). Anyone losing MIP coverage (including due to divorce or legal separation) may continue MIP coverage for up to 36 months in the MIP Continuation program, subject to these provisions:

1. MIP Continuation is priced without the World Bank Group subsidy.
2. Application for Continuation must be made within 60 days of the date of coverage loss, or MIP Continuation coverage will not be available.
3. Payment is due from (and coverage begins on) the first day of eligibility, regardless of when the application is accepted during the 60-day enrollment period.

4. If you obtain other health insurance during the 60-day period, you are not eligible to apply for MIP Continuation.
5. Normally, a dependent or terminating employee is covered under the Active Staff MIP of Retiree MIP through the end of the month of the coverage loss event (e.g., divorce).
6. MIP Continuation must occur in the same Plan (e.g., Retiree Plan 1, Active Staff Plan A, etc.) as prior to the MIP Continuation.
7. Individuals covered by MIP Continuation cannot switch Plans (e.g., Retiree Plan 1 to Retiree Plan 2, or Plan A to Plan B) while on MIP Continuation.
8. Individuals covered by MIP Continuation cannot switch Administrators (e.g., Aetna to Vanbreda) while on MIP Continuation. Note that Aetna provides billing services for all MIP Continuation participants, even those enrolled with Vanbreda.
9. MIP Continuation is closed to new entrants. In other words, any enrolled coverage plan (Individual, Dual or Family) cannot be increased during the MIP Continuation coverage period. (For example, someone on an MIP Continuation Individual plan cannot insure a spouse upon marriage or remarriage.)
10. Coverage cannot increase upon MIP Continuation relative to coverage under the Active Staff or Retiree MIP (i.e., changing from Individual coverage in the Active Staff MIP to Dual coverage in MIP Continuation is prohibited). However, if anyone entering MIP Continuation is pregnant at the time of application, MIP Continuation can be purchased to cover the pending birth, i.e. dual coverage for a pregnant individual entering MIP Continuation from the Active Staff MIP.
11. MIP Continuation can decrease relative to coverage under the Active Staff MIP. For example, an employee with Dual coverage in the Active Staff MIP can apply for Dual coverage or Individual coverage (but not Family coverage) in MIP Continuation. (This generally does not apply to the Retiree MIP).[1]

---

1. The exception is staff who terminate for cause such as misconduct o'r fraud. In such cases, MIP Continuation eligibility is at the discretion of the World Bank Group.

12. If someone enters MIP Continuation not pregnant, and becomes pregnant during the MIP Continuation coverage, the newborn(s) would be insured for the first 60 days of life under the mother's coverage; however, the newborn(s) would only be insured thereafter if the MIP Continuation was in the Family plan at the time of application.
13. Coverage remains in effect until the participant fails to pay the monthly premiums or 36 months, whichever is soonest. Payment failure includes late payments of premiums, non-payment of premiums, or checks returned for insufficient funds.
14. All checks must be paid in U.S. dollars.
15. As premiums are periodically adjusted, the cost of the MIP Continuation coverage will also adjust.
16. Payment collection and administration are performed on behalf of the World Bank Group by Aetna Individual Billing Unit. Each participant must provide and maintain with Aetna an accurate billing address for the monthly premiums.
17. Prepayment to Aetna for coverage is permitted. However, prepayment does not protect against premium increases.

Unlike Active Staff and Retiree MIP premiums, premiums for MIP Continuation are not subsidized by the World Bank Group. To find the current monthly MIP Continuation premium schedule, please go to http://go.worldbank.org/XZWKP9K6M0 and select information for spouses or retirees.

Active Staff MIP (Effective 1/1/2011)				**Retiree MIP (Effective 1/1/2011)**	
Coverage	Option A	Option B	Option C	Plan 1	Plan 2
Individual 1	$448	$342	$448	$522	$443
Dual	$808	$618	$808	$1044	$886
Family	$1080	$818	$1080	$1305	$1108
Family Plus	$1392	$1064	$1392	n/a	n/a

To enroll in MIP Continuation, the insured must complete the application form provided by the World Bank Group, and submit it with a check made payable to "IBRD" for the initial monthly amount to

Aetna at the address on the form. Checks that do not clear result in immediate cancellation of coverage with no opportunity to reapply (furthermore, the insured will be financially responsible for any claims filed between the end of any current coverage and the date the Bank Group cancels MIP Continuation coverage for non-payment.

Questions: Direct all billing and enrollment questions to Aetna Individual Billing Administration at (800) 429-9526 or (813) 775-0190. The fax number is (859) 280-1266
Email is memberiba@aetna.com.

For additional information, contact the HRD Operations via email (hroperations@worldbankgroup.org).

Index